SITTING FOR EQUAL SERVICE

LUNCH COUNTER SIT-INS,
United States, 1960s

MELODY **HERR**

 TWENTY-FIRST CENTURY BOOKS ▪ MINNEAPOLIS

Twenty-First Century Books
A division of Lerner Publishing Group, Inc.
241 First Avenue North
Minneapolis, MN 55401 U.S.A.

Website address: www.lernerbooks.com

Library of Congress Cataloging-in-Publication Data

Herr, Melody.
     Sitting for equal service : lunch counter sit-ins, United States, 1960s / by Melody Herr.
        p.   cm. — (Civil rights struggles around the world)
     Includes bibliographical references and index.
     ISBN 978–0–8225–8970–9 (lib. bdg. : alk. paper)
     1. African Americans—Civil rights—History—20th century—Juvenile literature. 2. Civil rights
movements—Southern States—History—20th century—Juvenile literature. 3. Southern States—Race
relations—Juvenile literature. I. Title.
     E185.61.H54 2011
     323.1196'073—dc22   2009049129

Manufactured in the United States of America
1 – CG – 7/15/10

CONTENTS

COFFEE PARTY

On February 1, 1960, four young men walked into the Woolworth's store in downtown Greensboro, North Carolina. Salesclerks probably thought they were typical college students, shopping for school supplies. That was only partly correct. Ezell Blair Jr., Franklin McCain, David Richmond, and Joseph McNeil were indeed students at the nearby Agricultural and Technical College (A&T). But that day, they hadn't come to Woolworth's merely to shop. They had come to win equality.

(Left to right) David Richmond, Franklin McCain, Ezell Blair Jr., and Joseph McNeil began their sit-in at the Woolworth's lunch counter in Greensboro, North Carolina, on February 1, 1960. In this photo, they have just left Woolworth's after the first day of the sit-in.

After buying a few items, the students sat at the lunch counter and ordered coffee and doughnuts. The waitress replied that she couldn't serve them. Blair showed her his receipts. Clerks in other departments had waited on him. Why, then, weren't he and his friends welcome here? Woolworth's manager, called to the scene, explained the lunch counter was reserved for white customers. In a fatherly tone, he tried to persuade the students to return to campus.

The four young men politely refused to leave until they received service. For the rest of the afternoon, they sat at the empty counter. When the store closed, they promised to return the next day and resume their protest.

Woolworth's wasn't the only business that denied blacks equal treatment. Throughout the southern United States, a long-standing tradition of segregation, known as Jim Crow, prohibited blacks from sharing public spaces—schools, swimming pools, hotels, hospitals, and other facilities—with whites. Jim Crow included a particularly strong taboo against whites and blacks sitting down and eating together.

The Thirteenth Amendment to the U.S. Constitution had ended slavery in 1865. Supreme Court rulings and federal legislation in the 1940s and 1950s had promised African Americans equality in education, employment, and politics. Yet segregation and other forms of racial discrimination daily reminded blacks that they were second-class citizens. Their civil rights existed only on paper. The time had come for more powerful tactics, the tactics of nonviolent protest.

That day in February 1960, the four young men from A&T College used a nonviolent protest, the sit-in. News of the "Greensboro Coffee Party" spread quickly, triggering sit-ins at segregated lunch counters throughout the South. At the same time, Blair, McCain, Richmond, and McNeil inspired thousands of fellow students—both black and white—to join the struggle for equality. The moment the Greensboro Four walked into the Woolworth's store was a heroic one in the U.S. civil rights movement.

CHAPTER 1

THE GREENSBORO FOUR

> Greensboro was a rather ambivalent community. I think it was a city that wanted to be known for being liberal, on the one hand, and cautious on the other, in terms of how far [citizens] really wanted to go."
>
> —Willa B. Player, President of Bennett College, 1979

The citizens of Greensboro took pride in their city. Founded in 1810 and located in Guilford County in the northern-central part of North Carolina, Greensboro was a prosperous business and cultural center. By 1960 it hosted Burlington Industries and Cone Mills, two of the biggest names in the textile industry. Several other textile manufacturers operated factories nearby. Greensboro companies produced machinery, concrete, steel, lumber, paint, chemicals, fertilizer, and feed for livestock. Print shops, foundries, bakeries, dairies, and hatcheries completed the list of local industries. A few national companies such as Coca-Cola, General Electric, and Kraft Foods had set up branches in the area. In addition, Greensboro served as headquarters for a number of insurance companies.

These thriving businesses attracted workers, and the city's population leapt from 59,000 residents in 1940 to nearly 75,000 in 1950 and continued to rise. In response, the city extended the water

Downtown Greensboro in 1945

and sewer lines, constructed new fire stations, added public housing units, and expanded the parks. By the mid-1950s, Greensboro had four hospitals and a public library system with a bookmobile (a traveling library). The city funded the public school system so well that Senior High School built a football stadium with seating for 10,500 spectators and a gym with seating for 4,800. Greensboro also hosted five colleges. For recreation, city residents could enjoy a number of public parks. Gillispie Park featured a golf course; Lindley Park had a swimming pool; and Greensboro Country Park offered a zoo as well as lakes for swimming, boating, and fishing.

Greensboro was not an isolated southern city. In the mid-1950s, it boasted two daily newspapers, four radio stations, and two television stations. Local movie theaters played foreign films as well as American box-office hits. As a symbol of their modern outlook, Greensboro's citizens pointed to the Tri-City Airport, which had provided mail service since 1928 and passenger service since 1930.

Just as citizens considered the airport evidence of a far-sighted willingness to adopt new technology, they considered peaceful race relations evidence of their modern social views. These views, they felt, were grounded in the ideals of liberty and democracy. Greensboro was named for the Revolutionary War hero General Nathanael Greene, who had fought the British at the Battle of Guilford

Greensboro was named for Nathanael Greene, a Revolutionary War hero who led U.S. troops to victory at the nearby Battle of Guilford Courthouse in 1781.

Courthouse in 1781. The Guilford Courthouse National Military Park, with a statue of General Greene at the entrance, was established near the city in the early twentieth century.

Greensboro was the scene of two other episodes in Americans' struggle for freedom. The Friends, a religious sect also known as the Quakers, had settled in Guilford County and forbade their members from owning slaves. In 1816 the Friends started manumission societies to work for the end of slavery. Although the manumission movement in North Carolina lasted only twenty years, the Friends drew attention to the injustice of slavery. Then around 1830, Vestal Coffin and Levi Coffin, two cousins who lived in Guilford County, created a system called the Underground Railroad for assisting escaping slaves. As the slaves fled north to Canada, where slavery was illegal, volunteer "conductors" guided them from hiding place to hiding place. The Underground Railroad quickly expanded across the nation. It carried hundreds of slaves to freedom before the outbreak of the U.S. Civil War in 1861.

DISCRIMINATION

In 1960, when Ezell Blair Jr. and his friends were A&T freshmen, Greensboro's civic leaders interpreted the ideals of liberty and democracy in their own way. African Americans were permitted to vote and participate in local politics, but their limited representation in city government was a measure of racial inequality. More than 25 percent of Greensboro's population was African American. But only one of the seven city council members and one of the seven school board members were black. Furthermore, blacks could not fully enjoy their city. The best jobs, the best schools, and the best parks were closed to them.

Citizens who wanted to think of Greensboro as progressive downplayed racial inequality. A history of the city, published in 1955, illustrated this attitude. The author, Ethel Stephens Arnett, devoted nearly five hundred pages to praise for Greensboro's industries, public facilities, and leisure activities. Yet she seldom mentioned a common feature throughout the city: the segregation of blacks and whites.

As these statistics from the U.S. Census Bureau show, black Americans faced inequalities in income and education in 1960.

Population

Total: 180,671,000

White: 160,023,000

Black: 20,648,000

Median Income

All families: $5,620

White families: $5,835

Black families: $3,230

Education: High School Graduate or More

Total percentage of U.S. population aged 25 years or older: 41.1%

Percentage of white persons aged 25 years or older: 43.2%

Percentage of black persons aged 25 years or older: 20.1%

Education: College Graduate or More

Total percentage of U.S. population aged 25 years or older: 7.7%

Percentage of white persons aged 25 years or older: 8.1%

Percentage of black persons aged 25 years or older: 3.1%

NORTH CAROLINA STATISTICS IN BLACK AND WHITE, 1960

According to data from the U.S. Census Bureau, on average North Carolina's black citizens had lower incomes and less education than the state's white citizens in 1960.

Population

Total: 4,556,155

White: 3,399,285

Nonwhite: 1,156,870

Median Income, Families Living in Urban Areas

All families: $4,843

White families: $5,565

Nonwhite families: $2,599

Education: Median Years of School Completed for Persons Aged 25 Years or Older

White: 9.8 years

Nonwhite: 7.0 years

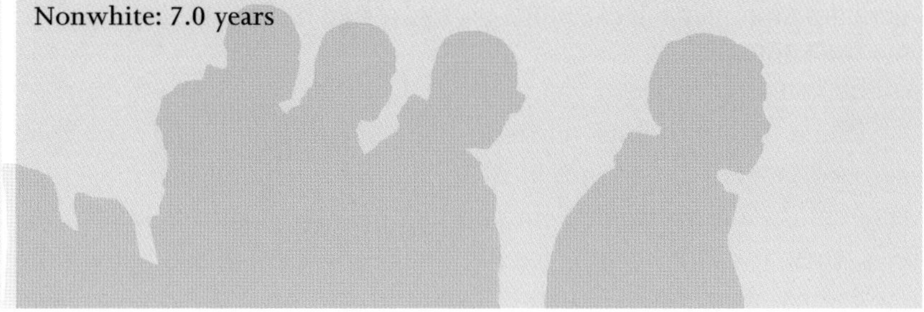

She remarked upon the city's few nonsegregated institutions, such as a school for children with cerebral palsy. She failed to point out that, except as maids or bellboys, African Americans were not welcome at the elegant hotels and restaurants described in the book. Instead, as if segregated facilities were special gifts to the black community, Arnett noted that certain parks, libraries, and hospitals were "for Negroes."

Many black citizens of Greensboro enrolled at A&T College after graduating from high school. The four friends—Blair, McCain, McNeil, and Richmond—lived in the college's Scott Hall, shown in this photo from the 1960s.

While many white citizens of Greensboro could overlook segregation, the four friends at A&T had faced it every day since they were children. Blair and Richmond had grown up in Greensboro. As boys, they attended schools for African Americans. If they joined the Boy Scouts, they joined an all-black troop and used the campground reserved for African Americans. If their families wanted to have a picnic, they went to Nocho Park because blacks were barred from Greensboro Country Park and many other recreational areas. If a boy's grandmother needed medical care, she was taken to L. Richardson Memorial Hospital for blacks or to the all-black ward at Cone Memorial Hospital.

As teenagers, when Blair and Richmond wrote term papers, they had to borrow books from the Carnegie Negro Library. When they wanted to swim, they had to use the pool at the Hayes-Taylor YMCA. When they took a date to the movies, they had to sit in the balcony, in seats designated for blacks. They went to Dudley, a high school for African Americans; then they enrolled at A&T, a college for blacks.

What did these young men have to look forward to after graduation? They might not have been able to recite the exact statistics, but they certainly knew that the average income in Greensboro's African American community was lower than the average income in the white community. They knew that a large percentage (40 percent) of black workers had service jobs and a comparatively small percentage (15 percent) had professional jobs. Of the 140 physicians in Greensboro in 1955, for example, only seven were African American. Most of the large companies in the city refused to hire African Americans for skilled jobs. Eager to maintain segregation, Cone Mills went so far as to set up a separate factory for black workers. However, owners of small businesses proved more willing to hire black mechanics and put blacks and whites side by side on the shop floor.

NORTH CAROLINA
AGRICULTURAL AND TECHNICAL COLLEGE

At a time when most southern universities closed their doors to blacks, North Carolina Agricultural and Technical College (A&T) offered Ezell Blair Jr. and his friends the opportunity to earn a college diploma. Like many U.S. colleges founded in the late nineteenth century, A&T was dedicated primarily to teaching farming and industrial trades. The institution taught the basic sciences and liberal arts as well. When the four friends enrolled in 1959, they could choose any one of fifty-five majors. A&T also offered a nursing program, two Reserve Officers' Training Corps programs, a school of engineering, and a graduate school.

Ezell Blair Jr. *(center)* and Joseph McNeil *(left)*, roommates at A&T, discuss their sit-in with Dr. George Simkins *(right)*, president of the local branch of the black civil rights organization, the National Association for the Advancement of Colored People (NAACP).

THE FOUR FRESHMEN

Ezell Blair Jr. was the shortest of the four friends by at least six inches (fifteen centimeters). With his clean-shaven face and huge grin, he also appeared to be the youngest, although he was eighteen years old. As a high school student, this outgoing youth had joined the science club, served as president of the school band, and earned membership in the National Honor Society. "Junior" Blair wasn't the first person in his family to attend college. Both of his parents had earned college degrees, and both were schoolteachers. Like many fellow college students, Junior Blair took odd jobs, such as house painting, during the summer to earn tuition money. At A&T, he was studying to become a lawyer.

The tallest of the four friends, Franklin "Frank" McCain towered a half foot (fifteen cm) above the others. This quiet eighteen-year-old wore glasses and, despite his height, did not play sports. McCain had come from Washington, D.C. At A&T, he was studying biology and chemistry. He and Junior Blair lived in the same dormitory, Scott Hall.

David Richmond, aged seventeen, had also grown up in Greensboro and had attended Dudley High School. A slender young man of medium height, he was considering a career as a minister.

Joseph "Joe" McNeil had received an academic scholarship and chosen to major in physics. He was a handsome seventeen-year-old with a carefully trimmed mustache. McNeil had grown up in

Franklin McCain *(left)* **and David Richmond** *(right)* **were both freshmen at North Carolina Agricultural and Technical College in 1960.**

Wilmington, North Carolina. When he arrived at A&T, he was assigned to a room with Blair in Scott Hall. Blair introduced him to Richmond and McCain. The four immediately became friends. They spent many evenings together, discussing current events and politics.

During the friends' freshman year, there were plenty of topics for informed college students to discuss. The peoples of Africa and Asia, who had suffered under European rule, were demanding independence. The world map changed almost overnight as former colonies became self-governing nations. The United States, the defender of democracy, competed for the allegiance of these new nations with the Union of Soviet Socialist Republics (USSR), the champion of Communism. This tense global rivalry was known as the Cold War. Meanwhile, at home, many U.S. citizens were beginning to ask if their society was truly democratic. And no one had more reason to question the reality of U.S. democracy than the African Americans who faced discrimination in education, housing, and employment.

Racial discrimination was not an abstract world problem for Blair, McCain, Richmond, and McNeil. It was a daily experience. It afflicted even college students, even in Greensboro, North Carolina.

■ ■ ■ LEADERSHIP IN THE BLACK COMMUNITY

Blair and his friends certainly knew college-educated neighbors working as janitors or porters because employers refused to hire African Americans for more prestigious jobs. Yet as the friends discussed such discrimination, they could also point to examples of African Americans who kept their dignity despite the injustice of segregation. Teachers, ministers, and parents tried to instill black youth with a sense of self-worth. At the same time, through schools, churches, and civic groups, Greensboro's African American leaders forged a sense of community and purpose.

Black citizens took pride in the high-quality education they gave their children. Greensboro operated a segregated school system, with one set of buildings and teachers exclusively for white students and another set of buildings and teachers exclusively for black students. Although the city school board gave white schools the lion's share of the funding, African American administrators were committed to improving their schools. By the early 1950s, when Blair, McCain, and Richmond were in elementary school, six black elementary schools in Greensboro were accredited. This was an impressive number, considering that only four other black elementary schools in the entire state of North Carolina were accredited. Dudley High School, too, had a national reputation for excellence.

> "And we all [the Greensboro four] respected each other. So it was likeone of those once-in-a-lifetime relationships."
> —Ezell Blair Jr., 1979

To a large extent, teachers deserved credit for these achievements. Every one of the teachers in Greensboro's black school system had a bachelor's degree; many of them had a master's degree as well. Most important, they were dedicated not only to teaching reading, writing, and arithmetic but also to showing students that African Americans could resist discrimination. For example, Vance Chavis taught physics at Dudley for many years. He also explained the importance of voting to his students and encouraged them to spread the word to their parents. Objecting to segregation, he refused to ride the segregated city buses. Once, during the 1930s, he urged students to join a boycott of segregated theaters. Nell Coley, an English teacher at Dudley, used class discussions to help students see their own potential and to challenge them to excel. Junior Blair's father, Ezell Blair Sr., the shop teacher, openly spoke out against racial injustice. His example had a strong influence on his students as well as on his son.

Professors at Greensboro's two black colleges likewise encouraged their students to seek equality. Edward Edmonds, a sociology professor at Bennett College for Women, protested the segregation of Greensboro's schools and parks. When Martin Luther King Jr., who was gaining a reputation as a civil rights leader, came to Greensboro in 1958, the president of Bennett invited him to preach in the college chapel. At A&T a graduate of the college who worked in the library told the students she met about her efforts to help end segregation on buses in the late 1940s. An A&T professor offered a class on African history so that students could learn how other peoples of color were winning their freedom. Junior Blair enrolled for this class. Students at A&T also read a volume of writings by black intellectuals compiled by the black poet Langston Hughes.

> **"You found persons with college educations running elevators."**
>
> —Jo Jones Spivey, Greensboro journalist reflecting on race-based job discrimination in the 1950s

Many of Greensboro's black leaders belonged to the National Association for the Advancement of Colored People (NAACP; pronounced "N-double A-C-P"). Professor Edmonds and Ezell Blair Sr. were NAACP members. So was Otis Hairston, the minister at Shiloh Baptist Church, which two of the four friends attended. As president of the Greensboro branch of the NAACP, Dr. George Simkins set an example by working for desegregation of the city's hospitals, schools, tennis courts, and golf courses. The Greensboro NAACP also hosted a youth group that held weekly meetings at a local black church or black college.

As a national organization, the NAACP linked African Americans across the United States and helped them to see their individual efforts as part of a common struggle for equality. The group looked to the courts and politics to bring equality to the African American community. Victory seemed far away to the four A&T freshmen, however.

In January 1960, back from the holiday break, McNeil reported to his friends yet another experience with segregation. He had gone to New York during the holidays. On the trip home, when he arrived at the Greensboro bus terminal, he had been denied service at the food counter. McNeil and his friends decided they had talked enough. The time had come to take action.

CHAPTER 2

MAKING
PROGRESS

"No State shall make or enforce any law which shall abridge the privileges or immunities of citizens of the United States; nor shall any State deprive any person of life, liberty, or property, without due process of law; nor deny to any person within its jurisdiction the equal protection of the laws."

—U.S. Constitution, Amendment 14, Section 1

As Junior Blair and his friends debated what action to take, they could look back over African Americans' long struggle for freedom and equality. In the historical record, they could see victories that had been won by political and legal tactics.

AMENDING THE CONSTITUTION

President Abraham Lincoln signed the Emancipation Proclamation, which officially freed slaves in certain states, on January 1, 1863. But no slaves were actually set free because the proclamation was issued during the Civil War. The war had begun in 1861 when a group of Southern states seceded (withdrew) from the United States of America (the Union) and created a separate nation of their own, which they called the Confederate States of America (the Confederacy). Lincoln's proclamation applied only to the slaves in those rebellious Southern states. Confederate leaders, of course, paid no attention to a law issued by the president of the United States.

This photo shows the capitol building in Richmond, Virginia. Richmond was the capital of the Confederacy during the Civil War (1861–1865).

On January 1, 1863, in the middle of the Civil War, President Abraham Lincoln issued the Emancipation Proclamation. It did not, in fact, free any slaves because it applied only to the states that were fighting the Union—which, therefore, ignored orders given by the U.S. president. Nonetheless, the Emancipation Proclamation made clear that slavery was a key issue in the war.

> [O]n the first day of January, in the year of our Lord one thousand eight hundred and sixty-three, all persons held as slaves within any state or designated part of a state, . . . in rebellion against the United States, shall be then, thenceforward, and forever, free; and the Executive Government of the United States, including the military and naval authority thereof, will recognize and maintain the freedom of such persons. . . .
>
> —[signed by] Abraham Lincoln

In this painting by American artist Francis Bicknell Carpenter, President Abraham Lincoln (*third from left*) reads the Emancipation Proclamation to his cabinet (advisers) before presenting it to the public.

African Americans, including children, continued to pick cotton in the American South in the 1890s.

In 1865 the Union army defeated the Confederate army and the Southern states began the process of rejoining the United States. rejoining the United States. This process was called Reconstruction. That same year, the Thirteenth Amendment was added to the U.S. Constitution. The amendment prohibited slavery in every part of the United States and its territories. All the slaves were set free.

However, many states, especially those in the South, refused to grant freed men and women the rights of full citizenship. Southern lawmakers passed so-called Black Codes, restricting African Americans to jobs as servants and farm laborers. In some cases, these laws forbade them to carry weapons, testify in court, and own property. Clearly, the Thirteenth Amendment had failed to safeguard the civil and political rights of African Americans, so Congress proposed another constitutional amendment.

The Fourteenth Amendment, ratified (passed) in 1868, did not mention race specifically. But it was clearly intended to force state governments to recognize the citizenship of all blacks. First, the amendment asserted that every person "born or naturalized in the United States" was a U.S. citizen. No state government could violate a citizen's rights or deny any person "equal protection of the laws." Second, the amendment gave every male citizen age twenty-one or older the right to vote. (No women were allowed to vote at this time.)

The amendment also outlined the penalty for failure to comply with these decrees. If a state government denied the voting rights of a particular group, the state's representation in Congress would be reduced by the same percentage as that group's percentage of the state's population. In other words, if 60 percent of the men of voting age in Mississippi were black and they were turned away from the polls, then Congress would turn away 60 percent of Mississippi's representatives.

Despite this penalty, some state governments tried to find ways to prevent African American men from voting. One more constitutional amendment was needed. This time Congress spelled out the demand for political rights. The Fifteenth Amendment, ratified in 1870, specified

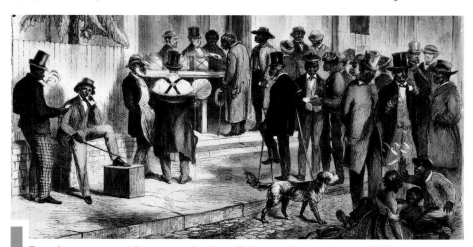

Freedmen were able to vote in New Orleans, Louisiana, in 1867. It took the Fourteenth and Fifteenth amendments to the U.S. Constitution to convince other states in the United States to grant African Americans the right to vote. Illustrations like this one from that time period often used racial stereotypes and caricatures in depicting black people.

that no citizen could be denied the right to vote "on account of race, color, or previous condition of servitude."

SEGREGATION

Despite the new constitutional amendments guaranteeing their rights, African Americans throughout the United States continued to face discrimination in education, housing, and employment. Discrimination was particularly harsh in the South, where racism took the form of segregation. Segregation laws—sometimes called Jim Crow laws—banned blacks from parks, libraries, golf courses, and other public places. On buses, in hospitals, and in movie theaters, segregation placed an invisible fence between whites and blacks.

The federal government did nothing to protect African Americans from segregation. In fact, in 1896, the U.S. Supreme Court ruled in the case *Plessy v. Ferguson* that segregation didn't violate the rights of

PLESSY v. FERGUSON

In 1890 Louisiana passed a law requiring railroads to provide "equal but separate" facilities for whites and for blacks. Homer Plessy, a black man, decided to test the law's constitutionality. In June 1892, he sat in a seat reserved for white passengers. He was arrested, and he went to court. A series of appeals eventually brought his case before the U.S. Supreme Court. In 1896 the court upheld Louisiana's segregation law because, Justice Henry Brown claimed, it did not violate the Fourteenth Amendment to the U.S. Constitution.

blacks as long as the facilities for them were equal to the facilities for whites. In other words, the court said that segregation itself was not racial discrimination. For decades afterward, this "separate but equal" doctrine was used to justify Jim Crow laws.

Undaunted, African Americans continued the struggle for equality. Black leaders generally believed that if they convinced a judge that segregation and other forms of discrimination violated their rights guaranteed by the U.S. Constitution, they would receive justice. If they persuaded Congress to pass antidiscrimination legislation, the law would protect them from the evils of racial prejudice. In 1909 black leaders founded the NAACP. Over the following decades, they coordinated their efforts to win justice using political and legal tactics.

CIVIL RIGHTS IN TIMES OF NATIONAL CRISES

During the Great Depression of the 1930s, when the U.S. stock market collapsed and many large banks failed, factories shut down and stores went out of business. Many Americans lost their jobs. Blacks, who often had the lowest-paying, most unstable jobs, were particularly hard hit by the Depression. The NAACP brought unemployment and racial discrimination to the attention of Congress and President Franklin D. Roosevelt.

In response, Roosevelt insisted that federal welfare and work relief programs provide assistance to all Americans, regardless of their skin color. He also appointed African Americans to important government posts and encouraged federal organizations to hire them. Setting a precedent for the nation, his administration ended the racial segregation of cafeterias and restrooms in federal buildings.

It took another crisis for the United States to take the next step toward racial equality. World War II began in 1939, when Germany invaded Poland. At first, the United States resolved to remain neutral. The United States sent aid to Great Britain, France, and neighboring nations with the hope that these Allies could fend off the combined force of the Axis powers—Germany, Italy, and Japan. Yet the war continued to expand across the globe. As Thanksgiving Day 1941 passed, observers wondered how much longer the United States would wait on the sidelines.

On December 7, 1941, Japan attacked the U.S. naval base at Pearl Harbor, Hawaii. The next day, the United States declared war on Japan. In turn, on December 11, Germany declared war on the United States. Suddenly, Americans found themselves fighting two wars: one in the Pacific and one in Europe. The nation's survival depended on the dedication of all citizens, from soldiers in the military to workers in the factories. As African Americans stepped forward, ready to serve, they rightfully demanded equality.

These U.S. Air Force pilots are part of the 99th Fighter Squadron, the first all-black unit to go into action in World War II.

African American women joined white women working in U.S. factories that made military supplies during the World War II.

Factories became federal workplaces of sorts during the war because corporations signed government contracts to produce planes, ships, tanks, and weapons. At first some defense industries refused to hire African Americans for highly paid, skilled jobs. Eager to prevent racial conflicts in wartime, President Roosevelt forbade discrimination in corporations with federal contracts.

Meanwhile, African Americans who served in the U.S. military had mixed experiences. In the marines and the navy, they found a variety of new positions opened to them. In the army, they could participate in officer-training programs alongside whites. Yet most of the half million black soldiers fought in segregated units, under the command of white officers. Their service, both on the European front and in the Pacific theater, contributed to the final victory of the United States and its allies in 1945.

Black war veterans and defense industry workers vowed to continue the struggle for equality in peacetime. They had proven their patriotism, and they believed they deserved the same treatment as other U.S. citizens. The new president, Harry S. Truman, seemed to agree. In 1946 he established the Civil Rights Committee to study racial issues. After the committee submitted a list of recommendations, he announced his support for ending segregation, safeguarding voting rights, and ensuring equal employment and housing opportunities. In 1948 he ordered the desegregation of the U.S. military.

When Truman issued this desegregation order, Americans were already facing another crisis: the Cold War between the Union of Soviet Socialist Republics (USSR) and the United States. The two

EXECUTIVE ORDER 9981

On July 26, 1948, President Harry S. Truman issued the following order, which created the Committee on Equality of Treatment and Opportunity in the Armed Forces and mandated desegregation of the U.S. military.

Whereas it is essential that there be maintained in the armed services of the United States the highest standards of democracy, with equality of treatment and opportunity for all those who serve in our country's defense. . . . It is hereby declared to be the policy of the President that there shall be equality of treatment and opportunity for all persons in the armed services without regard to race, color, religion or national origin.

—[signed by] Harry S. Truman

The United Nations—a global organization formed after World War II to promote world peace—adopted the Universal Declaration of Human Rights on December 10, 1948. Intended to protect all human beings around the world, this declaration emphasizes the right of every person—regardless of his or her skin color—to equal, just, and humane treatment. In the United States, segregation clearly violated the rights spelled out in the UN declaration. According to the declaration:

Article 1

All human beings are born free and equal in dignity and rights. . . .

Article 2

Everyone is entitled to all the rights and freedoms set forth in this Declaration, without distinction of any kind, such as race, colour, sex, language, religion, political or other opinion, national or social origin, property, birth or other status. . . .

Article 21

Everyone has the right to take part in the government of his country, . . . Everyone has the right to equal access to public service in his country. . . .

nations had fought side by side during World War II, but after the war, they began a contest for global power. They competed for military power—the most sophisticated weapons and the strongest army. Each nation also tried to prove that its own system of government was the best. The USSR stood for Communism. The United States stood for democracy.

The United States pointed to its soaring economy as proof that democracy was the best form of government for the people. In

Article 23

Everyone has the right to work, to free choice of employment, to just and favourable conditions of work and to protection against unemployment, . . . to equal pay for equal work.

Article 26

Everyone has the right to education. . . .

Article 27

Everyone has the right freely to participate in the cultural life of the community, to enjoy the arts and to share in scientific advancement and its benefits.

the 1950s, jobs were plentiful and wages were high. Around the country, more Americans—blacks included—owned cars, houses, and televisions. More people completed high school; more went to college. In the South, blacks as well as whites found opportunities in bustling factories and growing cities. In the midst of widespread prosperity, those who weren't victims of segregation could ignore the existence of racial discrimination. They could tell themselves that all citizens were equal.

The Soviets, however, pointed out the hypocrisy of Americans who treated African Americans as second-class citizens. According to Soviet propaganda, Communism—not democracy—offered real equality. This message could be damaging to the United States during the Cold War because most of the world's populations were peoples of color. They might be suspicious of alliances with the United States when they saw American racism. They might side with the USSR instead. A fear of alienating the dark-skinned peoples of other nations made some U.S. political leaders more sensitive to black Americans' calls for equality.

At the same time, fear of a Communist conspiracy at home threatened to silence such calls. Anyone who criticized the United States or questioned the status quo could be accused of working for the Communists. Although federal investigations uncovered a few Soviet spies, many loyal Americans had their careers destroyed by false accusations.

Afraid of being branded Communists, African American leaders avoided open protests against racial discrimination. During the 1950s, they used political and legal tactics to work for equality. The NAACP promoted voter registration. It lobbied for fair employment and

In the 1940s, the NAACP worked for equality through the courts. Posters in this NAACP office urge black Americans to join the organization.

housing laws. With noteworthy success, it also pressed lawsuits against violations of black citizens' constitutional rights. In response, the U.S. Supreme Court outlawed primary elections reserved exclusively for whites and ruled against segregation on interstate transportation.

CHALLENGING SEGREGATION IN SCHOOLS

Referring to the U.S. Constitution, NAACP lawyers built a strong case for black equality. The Fourteenth Amendment not only affirmed the citizenship of all persons born or naturalized (foreign-born person who fulfills requirements for U.S. citizenship) in the United States, it also guaranteed all persons "equal protection" of their lawful rights. But the backseats of the city bus were not equal to the front seats; the rear door of the movie theater was not equal to the main entrance. Most important, the worn textbooks and crumbling school buildings for black students were not equal to the newer books and school buildings for white students. In the United States, education was the gateway to success. Until all students received an equal education, they couldn't compete for jobs or other opportunities on an equal basis. Civil rights lawyers had another reason for targeting school segregation. They believed that if the Supreme Court ruled against segregated education, the entire legal structure of Jim Crow would collapse.

Perhaps civil rights leaders hoped integrated education would also eventually end racism. Giving every black child a sound education would help to break the stereotype of the illiterate black southern farmworker. At the same time, by sitting side by side in the classroom and playing together in the schoolyard, black children and white children would learn respect for one another. As adults, they would then overcome the prejudices that plagued U.S. society.

With these ambitious goals, Thurgood Marshall, head of the NAACP's Legal Defense and Education Fund, organized a set of lawsuits attacking segregated education. In the first stage of the attack, he and his fellow lawyers didn't challenge the "separate but equal" doctrine. They merely insisted that separate schools in fact be made equal. Lawyers reasoned that when taxpayers objected to the expense of duplicate systems, school districts would be forced to accept integration.

After a few winning cases in which the court affirmed black students' right to equal facilities, Marshall mounted the sec-ond stage of the attack. This time he argued that segregation itself violated students' rights. Even if their textbooks, cafeterias, and gyms were identical to those for white students, black students did not receive an identical education because segregation inflicted a feeling of inferiority. The judges agreed. In May 1954, in a cluster of cases collectively known as *Brown v. Board of Education*, the U.S. Supreme Court declared segregated education unconstitutional. Black—and white—Americans all over the country celebrated the NAACP's legal victory.

In the 1950s, Thurgood Marshall, a lawyer for the NAACP, brought cases against school segregation before the U.S. Supreme Court. His most successful case was *Brown v. Board of Education* (1954).

REACTION IN GREENSBORO

The day after the Court's declaration, members of the school board of Greensboro held their monthly meeting. The central topic of discussion, of course, was how they would respond to *Brown*. The members quickly reached an agreement. Rather than defy the Supreme Court, they announced that Greensboro's schools would follow the order to end segregation. Local newspapers and civic groups expressed support for the board's decision. A survey showed that city residents would accept desegregation.

The school superintendent, Benjamin Smith, took the first steps toward desegregation. On his roster, he began to list Greensboro's schools in alphabetical order, treating them as one group instead of dividing them into two categories, black and white. He insisted that black administrators and white administrators hold joint meetings. To prepare the school district's teachers for desegregation, he organized lectures and workshops on race relations. He also hired African Americans for jobs once reserved exclusively for whites.

By all appearances, Greensboro seemed prepared to set an example for the rest of the nation by offering black students a truly equal education. But if Junior Blair, Frank McCain, and David Richmond had expected to attend a high school where whites and blacks were classmates, they were mistaken. The African American citizens of Greensboro—along with other black citizens throughout the South—underestimated the power of racism. Segregationists fought to preserve the status quo with legal and political countertactics of their own.

CHAPTER 3

DEFENDING THE STATUS QUO

"[White citizens] should have sensed . . . that things were changing, that blacks were becoming more courageous . . . about these things that degraded them."

—Otis Hairston Sr., Greensboro resident, 1979

Desegregation. It wasn't a new word in 1954. The citizens of Greensboro had heard it before. But after the U.S. Supreme Court called for school desegregation, they couldn't agree on the word's definition. Did _desegregation_ mean all students riding the bus together, sitting together in the classroom, and eating together in the cafeteria? Did _desegregation_ mean black students using the same buildings as white students but attending separate classes and having lunch at separate tables? Exactly how many African American students were necessary to achieve desegregation? If a school had twenty-five hundred students and only four were black, could the school claim it was following the Court's order?

The first black students to enter Gillespie Elementary School in Greensboro sit at an assembly in August 1957.

For years, NAACP lawyers had pressed the courts to allow black students to attend schools with whites. At last, in 1954, in the case *Brown v. Board of Education*, the U.S. Supreme Court overturned the "separate but equal" principle by declaring segregated public schools unconstitutional. Contradicting the Court's previous ruling in *Plessy v. Ferguson* (1896), Chief Justice Earl Warren (*below*) made clear in his ruling that school segregation does indeed violate the Fourteenth Amendment and that segregation itself implies the inferiority of a racial group.

> In these days, it is doubtful that any child may reasonably be expected to succeed in life if he is denied the opportunity of an education. Such an opportunity, where the state has undertaken to provide it, is a right which must be made available to all on equal terms. . . .
> We conclude that, in the field of public education, the doctrine of "separate but equal" has no place. Separate educational facilities are inherently unequal. Therefore, we hold that the plaintiffs [those bringing the lawsuit] and others similarly situated for whom the actions have been brought are . . . deprived of the equal protection of the laws guaranteed by the Fourteenth Amendment.

Throughout the South, parents, school boards, NAACP lawyers, and state governors argued over the definition of desegregation. In North Carolina, the debate threatened to shut down the public schools. In Greensboro, despite the school superintendent's promise in May 1954 to obey the Supreme Court, five years later only a handful of black students attended school with white classmates. Students who dreamed of equality faced a disappointing reality as tradition, prejudice, and politics joined forces to maintain the racial status quo.

GOVERNOR HODGES AND JIM CROW

Luther Hodges became governor of North Carolina by default. Although he'd never held a political office, he was elected lieutenant governor in 1952 under William Umstead. When Governor Umstead died in the fall of 1954, Hodges instantly became the most powerful official in the state. Eager to keep his new position in the next election, Governor Hodges decided to turn school desegregation into a political issue. Assuming the majority of North Carolinians opposed it, he set out to win their votes. In the process, he deliberately ignited fear and put the education of all children—both black and white—in jeopardy.

Since Reconstruction, Southerners had resented the intervention of the federal government. Each state, they believed, should handle its own affairs. Following the lead of other southern politicians, Hodges insisted that educating the sons and daughters of North Carolina was the state's business. The U.S. Supreme Court had no right to interfere. Instead, Hodges proposed a plan to let the citizens of each school district decide the question of desegregation.

Luther Hodges became the governor of North Carolina in 1954.

This plan—named the Pearsall Plan after the state senator who chaired the special committee on education—offered two alternatives. First, a community could vote in favor of public school desegregation. In that case, if a white student (or his or her parents) objected, the state would pay tuition to a private school. Second, if citizens in a particular community couldn't agree on desegregation, they could vote to close the public schools. Hodges called this plan voluntary segregation, but in fact it was "voluntary" only for whites. Blacks couldn't apply for state tuition to a private school. If the school district shut down in order to prevent desegregation, African Americans couldn't attend the local public school either.

In addition to "voluntary segregation," Hodges adopted another euphemism for the Pearsall Plan: "the middle way." President Dwight D. Eisenhower had used the term to describe the path of compromise. For many North Carolinians, Hodges's proposal to close the schools didn't sound like a reasonable compromise. It sounded like a radical response. But Hodges framed the desegregation debate as a battle between two dangerous extremes. On one side, he claimed, stood the NAACP lawyers, ready to force white children to mingle with blacks. On the other side stood the Ku Klux Klan, ready to burn, bomb, and kill in defense of segregation. According to Hodges, the Pearsall Plan offered the middle way. He claimed to be the clearheaded governor North Carolinians needed to lead them safely along that road.

ACROSS THE COLOR LINE

By treating the desegregation debate as a crisis and presenting the Pearsall Plan as the only solution, Hodges won another term as governor. But it wasn't clear that the majority of North Carolinians were segregationists. For many white people who had grown up in a racially divided world, segregation was as natural as gravity. They moved through their lives without noticing it. Black people certainly noticed, but few whites understood their view because local segregation laws succeeded so well in keeping the two groups apart. Even citizens of the same town had little meaningful interaction across the color line.

The original Ku Klux Klan (KKK) was founded after the Civil War by southerners who felt threatened by newly liberated African Americans and who wanted to preserve white power. With the establishment of Jim Crow laws and other forms of racial discrimination, the KKK faded out in the late nineteenth century. When it was revived in the early twentieth century, members established local groups not only in the South but also in the West and the Midwest. This new Klan targeted blacks, immigrants, Catholics, and Jews—any minority group that seemed to challenge the dominance of white, American-born Protestants.

The KKK used terror and violence as its chief weapons. To show their strength and to intimidate minorities, Klansmen wearing long, hooded white robes gathered at night to burn crosses. On occasion, they beat and murdered individuals who dared to assert their rights.

The KKK remained active throughout the civil rights movement. In the twenty-first century, it is only one of several organizations calling for white supremacy.

True, a white businessman might hire a black janitor or say good morning to a black college professor. But he wasn't likely to choose a black man as a business partner or go golfing with him.

Open, violent racism was uncommon in Greensboro, where citizens valued courtesy and civility. White business and civic leaders typically treated blacks with paternalism. Assuming a fatherly role, these men felt it was their duty to watch over and care for African Americans who, supposedly, couldn't manage their own affairs. Caesar Cone, the owner of several local textile mills, exemplified this paternalistic attitude. Cone had developed an acquaintance with John Tarpley, the principal of Dudley High School (for blacks) and the supervisor of all local black schools. In the late 1930s, when the African American community wanted to build a YMCA, Tarpley had approached Cone and asked for financial assistance. Cone agreed to donate $50,000 for the construction of a YMCA if African Americans bought the land. When the building was finished, Cone named it the Hayes-Taylor YMCA in honor of two of his black servants, Sally Hayes and Andrew Taylor. Servants were most likely the only African Americans with whom Cone had daily contact.

Whereas paternalism may have appeared benevolent on the surface, it actually reinforced inequality by demanding that African Americans adopt a posture of deference. If Tarpley expected Cone to make a donation to the YMCA, for example, he couldn't confront him about job discrimination at the textile mills. Although by the early 1950s, Greensboro had one African American on the city council and another on the school board, these leaders had limited effectiveness. They felt they needed to cooperate with the white elite, even if they had to appear submissive, because whites held an unequal share of economic and political power. In the same way, black maids, chauffeurs, and gardeners took care not to offend their white employers.

Whites easily mistook this compliance for acceptance of the racial status quo. They failed to realize that blacks had to act that way in order to survive in a society where whites made the rules. Cone, for example, could congratulate himself for donating money for the new YMCA without truly understanding how blacks viewed segregation. Consequently, when the U.S. Supreme Court called for school desegregation in 1954, many whites refused to believe the local African American community supported the Court's order. They blamed the NAACP and other outsiders for causing trouble. In Greensboro, John Foster, the chairman of the school board, decided to take a survey of black opinion. He asked his domestic maid, his truck driver, and his janitor what they thought. Based on their answers, he concluded that the average black citizen didn't favor school desegregation. Foster apparently didn't consider that his employees might give him the answer they believed he wanted to hear.

Another reason white citizens in Greensboro dismissed the possibility of African American discontent was that, compared to other regions in the South, the city offered African Americans a great deal. African Americans had a hospital, a YMCA, and churches of their own. They had a solid school system and two colleges. Not only were they better educated than other black North Carolinians, according to the statistics,

A bus driver removes a Jim Crow sign from his bus in 1956 in Greensboro. The sign tells white riders to sit in the front, and African American riders to sit in the rear. Greensboro desegregated its buses that year.

they were better off economically. Furthermore, in the late 1940s, many government offices and downtown businesses had removed the Whites Only signs. At basketball and softball games, when a black team played against a white team, fans of both teams sat together in the bleachers. The YWCA was also experimenting with interracial meetings.

If Greensboro provided opportunities generally unavailable to African Americans in the South, why did school desegregation look so threatening to some white citizens? The racial codes of the Jim Crow South included long-standing taboos against intimacy of any sort. Blacks and whites were not supposed to swim in the same pool. They didn't shake hands or share meals. When members of the white YWCA first began inviting members of the black YWCA to meetings, the white women deliberately scheduled the joint sessions so as to avoid dining with the black women. If desegregation took place, children would violate every one of these taboos on a routine school day. When the children became adults, opponents of desegregation warned, they would ignore the prohibition against interracial marriage.

This warning alarmed some parents in North Carolina as much as it alarmed parents throughout the South. In general, however, citizens of the state resigned themselves to school desegregation. A newspaper editor who toured the state reported that the public was ready to comply with the *Brown v. Board* decision. In the county where Greensboro was located, sociologists found that only 18 percent of the population strongly opposed desegregation. Although only 18 percent strongly supported it, the majority seemed willing to obey the law. Desegregation was inevitable, these individuals believed. Defiance of the U.S. Supreme Court was foolhardy. The idea of her son going to school with a black child might be disagreeable to a white mother, but she was nonetheless prepared to accept the situation if necessary. During a survey conducted in May 1954, the editors of the Greensboro *Daily News* reached the same conclusion: most citizens were ready to accept the Court's ruling.

Ignoring evidence of North Carolinians' readiness to accept desegregation, Governor Hodges painted a picture of white mobs barring black children from the schools. His prediction of violence successfully persuaded voters that the Pearsall Plan was the only reasonable solution. As governor, he promised, he would defend the racial status quo. But Hodges also ignored evidence of black citizens' determination to win an equal education in desegregated schools.

THE STRUGGLE FOR SCHOOL DESEGREGATION

In late 1955, as the Greensboro School Board continued to postpone desegregation, African American families began to take action. As proof of their confidence in the political and legal tactics advocated by the NAACP, they joined the local chapter in record numbers, doubling its membership. Every month, African American parent-teacher associations (PTAs) sent representatives to school board meetings to demand that all students receive an equal education. The PTA representatives pressed for desegregation. They also called for better facilities at black schools in the belief that when Greensboro's taxpayers realized how expensive it was to maintain two separate, identical systems, they would consent to desegregation.

The struggle for a new gymnasium at Dudley High School illustrates both the black community's persistence and the school board's resistance. The Dudley gym wasn't long enough for a basketball court or wide enough to seat all the spectators. Therefore, the Dudley PTA asked for either a new building or permission to use the gym at Senior High, a school for whites. The board first suggested that Dudley's team play on the smaller court. Then the board claimed the Senior High gym was booked every night Dudley had a game. When the Dudley PTA offered to reschedule the games for dates the Senior High gym was free, the board finally agreed to let the black team play there. Soon after making this deal, the board approved plans for a new, larger gym at Dudley High School. The school board thought Greensboro's citizens would rather pay for a new building than permit anything resembling desegregation.

While PTA representatives carried on their lobbying efforts, African American families applied for student transfers. Under the Pupil Assignment Act passed by the North Carolina legislature in 1955, the local school board—not the state—decided which public school a student could attend. The new law listed a number of criteria for making this decision, including a student's home address and school record. Ostensibly, race was not one of the criteria. In practice, though, the law left enough room for a school board to justify assigning any student to any school. At the risk of losing their jobs and inviting harassment, black parents tried to enroll their children in exclusively white schools. Again and again, in Greensboro and throughout the state, local school boards turned down transfer applications.

For their safety, the first African American students to attend Greensboro's Gillespie Elementary School are escorted across campus in August 1957. Desegregation of public schools in the South sometimes became violent.

Meanwhile, North Carolina officials found another way to sidestep the U.S. Supreme Court's order to end school segregation. State officials claimed that, if a few white schools admitted a few black students, the school system was desegregated. This practice became known as "token desegregation." In Greensboro, when the 1957–1958 academic year began, five black students entered Gillespie Elementary (previously reserved for whites) and one black student, Josephine Boyd, entered Senior High. Every day, all year long, Boyd and her family faced harassment: punctured car tires, broken windows, anonymous midnight phone calls, attacks with eggs and stones.

Desegregation in Greensboro was relatively peaceful, however, in comparison to the violence in Little Rock, Arkansas, that same year. There, when a federal court demanded that the city's white schools admit black students, Governor Orville Faubus vowed to resist. He hoped to win votes by fighting desegregation, just as Governor Hodges did in North Carolina. Claiming a riot would break out if the nine

TOKEN **DESEGREGATION**

In the 1950s, if a segregated school admitted a single black student—even though all the other students were white—the school board could claim that it had followed the U.S. Supreme Court's order to end segregation. This effort to evade the law was known as "token desegregation" because it did not truly follow the spirit of the law.

Elizabeth Eckford *(front with books)* is followed by angry parents as she leaves Central High School in Little Rock, Arkansas, in 1957. Eckford was turned away from the school by National Guard troops under the direction of Arkansas governor Orval Faubus. The school was eventually forced to allow her and eight other African American students to attend.

African American students accepted at Little Rock's Central High were allowed to attend, Faubus ordered the Arkansas National Guard to barricade the school. As he predicted, segregationists formed a mob at Little Rock. The new students weren't able to enter Central High until mid-September, when President Eisenhower sent federal troops to lead them into the school. The president had hesitated for weeks. Hoping not to antagonize southern voters, he had refused to take a public stand on desegregation. But Faubus's defiance of federal authority forced Eisenhower to act. Federal troops stayed at Central High for two months, until the Arkansas National Guard, under federal control, took over the job of protecting the students. Despite their armed escorts, these young blacks endured prejudice and harassment.

■ ■ ■ ■ MEASURING PROGRESS

Meanwhile, back in Greensboro, Benjamin Smith, the school superintendent, had done what he could to achieve desegregation in the city's schools. In addition to holding workshops on race relations for school administrators and teachers, he had hired blacks for jobs traditionally reserved for whites. Yet he couldn't stop Governor Hodges's Pearsall Plan or prevent school board members from trying to bar black students from schools exclusively for white students. And even Smith's limited achievements sparked hostility. Opponents of desegregation burned crosses in his yard and smashed windows in his house. Undaunted, Smith postponed retirement in order to guide parents, teachers, and students through the 1957–1958 school year, the first year of desegregation.

That year, in Greensboro only six black students attended class with white students. But many believed that such token desegregation didn't count as true desegregation. Thousands of African American children still attended separate schools. The next academic year, 1958–1959, the number of token black students in white schools dropped from six to five. African American families recognized that the school board wanted to satisfy the U.S. Supreme Court's order with minimum compliance. State lawmakers and Governor Hodges had sided with the segregationists. Meanwhile, the federal government wavered. After the Little Rock crisis, President Eisenhower refused to enforce any more school desegregation orders. The Supreme Court agreed that local officials should define desegregation and set their own timetables for implementing it.

By late 1959, the political and legal tactics that African Americans had once used so effectively seemed useless. Opponents of equality had developed countertactics that had perverted democracy in the United States. The time had come, young African Americans decided, to try something new.

CHAPTER 4

SITTING DOWN
AT THE LUNCH COUNTER

"[T]hese young people had reached a point that they were a little bit weary of there being two standards. Now these, of course, were the children of men and women who had been in World War II. And I think that they had a different outlook, possibly, from that that their parents had had. And I think some of them wondered why this [the protest against segregation] had not been done long before, why they were having to do it."

—Jo Jones Spivey, Greensboro journalist, 1979

As A&T College students, Junior Blair, Frank McCain, David Richmond, and Joe McNeil discussed their daily confrontations with discrimination. They agreed that the time had come to put an end to it. The political and legal tactics advocated by the nation's black leaders had failed. Lobbying and lawsuits generated a great deal of talk, from politicians' speeches and newspaper articles to court proceedings and congressional legislation, but very limited results. The four friends decided that they wouldn't merely talk. They would take action.

FORMULATING A PLAN

The nine black teenagers who had entered Little Rock Central High School in 1957 in defiance of a hostile crowd of segregationists had demonstrated that young people could join the struggle for equality.

Some members of the Little Rock Nine spoke at A&T about their experience in high school integration. The Little Rock Nine are pictured here with civil rights activist Daisy Bates *(back row, second from right)* in the late 1950s.

Some of these courageous students gave a presentation to the Greensboro NAACP youth group. The example of the "Little Rock Nine" convinced the four A&T freshmen that they could make a difference. They began to plan how they could end segregation in Greensboro.

The friends chose the lunch counter at F. W. Woolworth's for their first effort. Located about 2 miles (3.2 kilometers) from campus, this department store in downtown Greensboro welcomed A&T students. Salesclerks in the toy department, the stationery department, and the housewares department happily waited on black customers. At the lunch counter, however, the waitress had orders from management not to serve African Americans. If they wanted something to eat, she was supposed to direct them to the store's snack bar, which had no stools. Blacks weren't permitted to sit at the counter with whites.

Woolworth's encouraged desegregation throughout the rest of the store, Frank McCain pointed out to his friends. Such arbitrary rules proved that racial discrimination was simply illogical. For this reason,

The Woolworth's store in Greensboro was desegregated everywhere but at the lunch counter, where blacks were not allowed to sit and eat.

the four friends decided the lunch counter would make the perfect site for a protest against segregation.

Next they had to choose their tactics. They could send a petition to the Greensboro City Council, write to Woolworth's headquarters in New York, or sue the company. But they believed that political and legal tactics weren't effective. They decided they would try nonviolent protest.

The concept of nonviolent protest in the United States wasn't new. More than 100 years earlier, in 1846, the U.S. writer Henry David Thoreau had refused to pay taxes in order to express disapproval of the war between the United States and Mexico. The United States, he claimed, wanted to conquer more territory for slaveholders. Although Thoreau's personal protest didn't attract much attention at the time, he wrote an essay three years later called "Civil Disobedience" about the need to protest injustice, even if one had to go to jail.

HENRY DAVID THOREAU'S "CIVIL DISOBEDIENCE" (1849)

In the 1840s, writer Henry David Thoreau made a personal protest against slavery and the war between the United States and Mexico by refusing to pay a tax. He was arrested and sent to prison. Thanks to a friend who paid the tax for him, Thoreau was released after a single night. This short stay, however, proved to him that peaceful civil disobedience was an effective tactic because it challenged authorities to respond.

In his essay "Civil Disobedience," Thoreau urged citizens to defy an immoral government and its unjust laws, even at the risk of going to prison. Perhaps the most famous sentence of this essay, which has inspired activists around the world, is "Under a government which imprisons any unjustly, the true place for a just man is also a prison."

In the early 1900s, Mohandas Gandhi provided another model of nonviolence when he led India's struggle for independence from Great Britain. A well-educated man with deep religious beliefs, Gandhi saw the ways in which the British exploited India's people. He resolved to bring an end to British rule in India. Instead of armed revolution, Gandhi advocated boycotts, labor strikes, and peaceful demonstrations.

MOHANDAS GANDHI, PIONEER OF NONVIOLENT PROTEST

Mohandas Karamchand Gandhi, known as Mahatma Gandhi, first encountered segregation while traveling in South Africa, where a conductor evicted him from a railroad car reserved for white passengers. Born in India in 1869, Gandhi had grown up in a middle-class family and attended law school in London. In 1893 he accepted a job as a lawyer in South Africa. There, he quickly discovered, the shade of his skin mattered more than his background and education. The British, who ruled India as well as parts of Africa at the time, treated all persons of color as inferior human beings. For more than twenty years, Gandhi fought for the rights of fellow Indians in South Africa, and he always insisted upon nonviolent tactics.

By the time Gandhi returned to India in 1915, he was a famous champion of peaceful protest. Yet his work had really just begun. When he saw the ways in which British colonial officials, landlords, and factory owners mistreated the Indian people, he tried to end oppressive taxes and win better wages. Eventually he joined the movement for India's independence.

Rather than use guns against the British, Gandhi called for boycotts and peaceful labor strikes. He once made a personal pilgrimage, walking hundreds of miles. He often fasted, going without food for days. Several times he was sent to jail.

Thanks largely to his efforts, Great Britain granted India independence in 1947. When Gandhi was assassinated only a few months later, he was mourned around the world as a spokesman for nonviolent resistance to oppression. For Americans confronting racial discrimination, Gandhi offered not only a set of tactics but also a message of love for all human beings and a willingness to suffer for a just cause.

In 1947 Gandhi's efforts helped India's people gain independence from Great Britain, without an armed revolution. They were less successful, however, at maintaining peace among themselves. Ignoring Gandhi's plea for a united country, Hindu leaders and Muslims leaders turned the former British colony into two new nations: India and Pakistan. Violence immediately erupted between the two groups. In early 1948, Gandhi was assassinated by a young man who blamed him for the bloodshed. Gandhi is remembered around the world as a spiritual leader and a pioneer of nonviolent protest.

Mahatma Gandhi (pictured here in 1946) was a champion of nonviolent resistance to oppression.

More recently, Martin Luther King Jr. had demonstrated the power of nonviolent protest when he led a bus boycott in Montgomery, Alabama. In Montgomery, as in many southern cities, African American passengers had to sit in the back of the bus. If the bus became crowded, blacks near the middle had to surrender their seats to white passengers. In December 1955, a middle-aged woman named Rosa Parks refused to give up her seat. When she was arrested, African American citizens organized a peaceful protest: they refused to ride segregated buses. For a year, they walked or joined carpools, while empty buses rolled down the streets. At last, in late December 1956, the U.S. Supreme Court overruled the city's bus segregation law. Black passengers won equality without guns, knives, or bombs.

Rosa Parks is fingerprinted after being arrested again for organizing a boycott in Montgomery, Alabama, on February 22, 1956. This was two months after Parks's refusal to give up her seat on the bus led to the boycott of the city's bus system.

African American residents of Montgomery, Alabama, walk to work during the Montgomery bus boycott in February 1956.

King and Gandhi inspired the four friends from A&T, especially Blair. He had watched a television program about India, and the pictures of British officers arresting Gandhi time and time again made a strong impression. Although Blair worried about upsetting his family, he decided that he would go to prison, if necessary, in order to win equality for African Americans. King's visit to Greensboro in 1958 had a similarly powerful effect on Blair, who heard King's sermon at Bennett College. King provided a living example of nonviolent leadership.

As Blair and his friends discussed Gandhi's protests in India and King's bus boycott in Montgomery, they developed a plan for their own protest at Woolworth's. They may have considered a boycott, but the loss of four customers wouldn't have hurt the company's profits. McNeil proposed the opposite: instead of boycotting Woolworth's, they would occupy it. They would sit down at the lunch counter and refuse to leave until the waitress served them.

It was a brilliant idea. Whether or not McNeil knew the history of labor unions, U.S. workers had pioneered the strategy, which came to be known as a sit-in. When striking workers refused to enter factories, employers often hired replacements to keep the machines running.

These General Motors employees in Flint, Michigan, staged a sit-in protest in 1937. It was the first successful sit-in in the United States. It set the stage for later sit-ins, such as the one the A&T students planned for the Greensboro Woolworth's store in 1960.

When Joe McNeil suggested that the four friends challenge segregation at Woolworth's, he selected a highly strategic site for the sit-in. If they'd held their protest at Macy's department store in New York, they couldn't have drawn more publicity than they did at the dime store in downtown Greensboro, North Carolina.

As a store offering things everyone needed and where everyone could afford to shop, Woolworth's was as American as apple pie. The company's diamond logo and signature red storefront appeared on Main Street in all major U.S. cities. Furthermore, the company's founder, Frank Winfield Woolworth, had exemplified the American dream. Born to a farm family in 1852, this visionary entrepreneur had set up a series of stores, stocked them with low-priced items, and experimented with new methods of retailing. Woolworth expanded his business empire until, at the time of his death in 1919, his company owned more than one thousand stores. The former farm boy left an estate worth $27 million, a vast fortune at that time.

Forty years later, with more than two thousand stores in the United States, and many overseas, Woolworth's was not only a familiar hometown American store but also a prosperous, international business. For this reason, when the four A&T freshmen sat down at the Woolworth's lunch counter in Greensboro, they sat down on a national—and global—stage. Other civil rights activists soon joined them at lunch counters and on picket lines at Woolworth's stores across the United States to protest segregation.

By sitting at the machines, however, workers prevented outsiders from taking their jobs. At the same time, they shut down the factories until management met the union's demands.

Blair pointed out to his friends that they might sit for months without getting service. Or the store manager might call the police. Or white customers might start a riot. Maybe everyone would simply ignore the black college students on the lunch counter stools. Nonetheless, on Sunday evening, January 31, 1960, Blair, McCain, Richmond, and McNeil made a pact to begin their nonviolent protest at the downtown Woolworth's the following afternoon.

FIRST ENCOUNTER

On Monday, February 1, the four friends met at the A&T library. McCain wore his Reserve Officers Training Corps (ROTC) uniform. Blair wore a suit and tie. Richmond and McNeil wore dress slacks and well-polished shoes. Together, they headed downtown.

On the way, they stopped at a small clothing store on East Market Street to inform the owner, Ralph Johns, of their plan. Although Johns wasn't black, he allied himself with Greensboro's African American community in the struggle for equality. At his store, he catered to black customers and

Ralph Johns, a business owner in Greensboro, talked to the A&T students before they staged the first day of the sit-in at the Woolworth's lunch counter. Johns was a supporter of their cause.

> "I would go to Woolworth's and Kress's to eat lunch, and I couldn't understand why I could sit down and eat, and yet the blacks had to stand up or take their food and leave. . . . I would go to the S&W or Mayfair Cafeterias and watch many of my black friends walk by the window where I sat eating, and yet they could not enjoy the same privilege as an American. . . . My conscience bothered me, and it broke my heart to see this indignity heaped on a human being of another color than white. . . . I decided to do something about this wrong."
>
> —*Ralph Johns, Greensboro businessman, 1979*

employed a black salesclerk. He belonged to the NAACP, recruited new members for the organization, and urged African Americans—especially college students—to stand up for their rights. He had earlier spoken with McNeil about protesting segregation. When McNeil and his fellow freshmen arrived that Monday afternoon, Johns led them to the back of his store. Excitedly, he listened to their plan. He promised to call local reporters and alert them that a big story was developing at the Woolworth's lunch counter. Greensboro's citizens, he believed, needed to know about racial discrimination in their own city. Johns also offered to pay bail if the young men were arrested.

Assured of Johns's support, the friends walked to South Elm Street. About four o'clock, they entered Woolworth's. After buying a few small items, they approached the lunch counter. The long L-shaped counter, running along two sides of the store and spiked with sixty-six stools, must have looked like an armed fortress to the nervous young men. They sat down and ordered coffee and doughnuts.

The waitress refused to serve the four friends because, as she reminded them, she wasn't allowed to wait on black people. They had prepared for this response. Showing her their receipts, they explained that other Woolworth's employees had waited on them. So, they asked, why couldn't she? Was the store a private club requiring each customer to carry a membership card? Or was the store truly open to the public? At a loss for answers to this barrage of questions, the waitress scurried away to get the manager, C. L. Harris.

A balding, middle-aged man who usually wore glasses and a gray suit, Harris took pride in his store. When he had started working for Woolworth's in 1923, all its merchandise cost ten cents or less. For this reason,

C. L. Harris was manager of the Woolworth's store in Greensboro during the lunch counter sit-ins in 1960.

Woolworth's was known as a "five and ten" or a "dime store." As the manager of the Greensboro branch, Harris attempted to improve Woolworth's status by selling more expensive goods, such as televisions and watches. He worked hard to keep his store in order. Rather than sit in his upstairs office giving orders, he came down to the sales floor to look over records, tidy displays, and greet customers. Harris didn't want any trouble that might spoil the reputation of his neat, well-run store.

Summoned by the waitress, Harris went to meet the four African American students demanding coffee. Politely, he tried to persuade them to leave. With the same politeness, they listened. But they refused to go. They vowed to stay until the store closed and to return in the morning to continue their sit-in. Harris decided to let them sit. Most likely, he hoped that they would get bored and move their protest elsewhere.

Meanwhile, a policeman arrived. Clapping his club in his hand, he paced behind the lunch counter stools. He was clearly angry. Yet McCain read perplexed anxiety on the man's face as well. If the students had threatened the waitress with weapons, the policeman would have immediately drawn his revolver. He'd never seen nonviolent tactics, however, and didn't know how to respond.

After watching the waitress, the manager, and the policeman fail to evict the students, the dishwasher decided to try. As an African American woman, she faced discrimination every day. She blamed a handful of troublemakers for stirring racial prejudices against decent folks like herself. Blacks, she believed, could succeed in a society controlled by whites only by working hard and carefully following the rules—even the Jim Crow rules. Protest of any sort against the status quo was dangerous because it could spark hostility. The dishwasher certainly wasn't the only African American in Greensboro who thought this way. Worried that the sit-in could put her own job in jeopardy, she scolded the four friends. They should know better, she said, than to demand service at a place reserved for white customers.

Two elderly white women had a surprisingly different reaction when they saw black students sitting at the lunch counter. Instead of scolding them, these two women congratulated them for challenging segregation. Meanwhile, other white customers, outraged that the young men dared to step out of line, called them nasty names.

Despite such taunts, Blair, McCain, Richmond, and McNeil felt their confidence grow every minute. They were men—black men—demanding their rights as Americans. Through nonviolent tactics, they were advancing the cause of African American equality.

After an eventful hour, the store closed and the four friends stood to leave. With a promise to return in the morning, they walked out the door and headed home. They arrived back at A&T to discover they'd become instant celebrities. A local radio station had reported the sit-in at Woolworth's, and the news electrified the entire campus. Fellow students rushed to volunteer for the sit-in the next day.

On the second day of the lunch counter sit-in, Joseph McNeil *(left)* and Franklin McCain *(second from left)* returned to the store, along with Billy Smith *(second from right)* and Clarence Henderson *(right)*.

"And it wasn't until [I went to college] that I really began to understand or see many of the barriers that were thrown up as far as the blacks were concerned, and the possibilities of then being able to do something. It just didn't dawn on me. . . . [T]his was the first time that I ever started really thinking about some of the injustices that were going on at the time."

—Robert Tyrone Patterson, former A&T student, 1989

■ RECRUITING SUPPORTERS

Blair and his friends welcomed this enthusiastic support, yet they realized that without some kind of coordination, the protest could quickly get out of hand. Wasting no time, they called together key student leaders. At an emergency meeting that night, A&T students created the Student Executive Committee for Justice to organize the sit-in. Eighteen students agreed to serve on the committee; Blair was named the chairman. The committee made clear that nonviolence was essential. During the sit-in, protesters must not speak angrily, use rude language, or fight back in any way, no matter how they were treated.

After laying the ground rules, the committee organized a schedule for the protest volunteers. By sitting in shifts, students could keep the stools at the lunch counter occupied without missing classes. The committee also arranged for transportation between the A&T campus and downtown Greensboro. For Blair in particular, it was a busy evening after a very exciting, very exhausting Monday afternoon.

The next morning at ten o'clock, the four friends made good on their promise to the Woolworth's manager. Accompanied by nearly thirty fellow students, they returned to the lunch counter and resumed the sit-in.

CHAPTER 5

AN **EXPLOSIVE** ENCOUNTER

"We didn't want to put the world on fire, we just wanted to eat. But behind [the sit-in], we . . . did have the idea that this would catch on. We were hoping it would catch on and it would spread throughout the country, but it went even beyond our wildest imagination."

—Ezell Blair Jr., 1979

On Tuesday morning, February 2, 1960, soon after Woolworth's manager C. L. Harris unlocked the doors, the A&T College students arrived. They walked to the lunch counter, sat on the stools, and ordered food. When the waitress refused to serve them, they opened books and started reading. They didn't argue with store employees. They didn't destroy merchandise. They didn't harass customers. They simply sat there, neatly dressed, quietly studying. From time to time, another group of students came to take the seats of those who had to return to campus for classes.

Harris couldn't complain about the students' conduct. He only wished they hadn't chosen to protest segregation at his lunch counter. Before the end of the week, his Woolworth's store became the center of racial tensions in Greensboro. It also became the center for a wave of sit-ins spreading from North Carolina to Florida. In cities all over the South, young black men and women adopted nonviolent protest as a powerful new tactic in the struggle for equality.

A&T students continue to participate in the sit-in at the Wooworth's lunch counter in Greensboro in February 1960. The sit-in movement soon spread across the South.

◼ WEEK ONE

A&T students continued the sit-in at the Greensboro Woolworth's until closing time on Tuesday. On Wednesday, when the store opened, they returned again. As the news spread, more volunteers joined the sit-in. By Thursday, there weren't enough stools for all the protesters, and a group headed to the lunch counter at the downtown S. H. Kress store.

Also on that Thursday, a pack of white teenagers appeared at the Woolworth's lunch counter. These young men were known as ducktails because of their hairstyle: slicked down on the top and sides, with a ridge in the back combed upward like a bird's tail. In contrast to the neatly dressed students, these young men wore jeans and leather jackets. In the 1950s and 1960s, this hairstyle and these clothes were considered symbols of youthful rebellion. While the student protesters sat at the lunch counter reading, the white youths taunted and harassed them. The protesters, committed to nonviolence, didn't fight back. When one of the bullies tried to set a protester's coat on fire, he was arrested. The police, who were keeping the sit-in under surveillance, arrested two more of the bullies the same day.

These white men sat at the counter at the Greensboro Woolworth's to prevent black students from continuing their sit-in.

Approximately 400 college students participated in the sit-in in Greensboro on February 6, 1960.

The turnout of African American students from Bennett College and Dudley High School that first week pleased the four friends but didn't surprise them. It merely proved what they'd known all along: other young blacks resented segregation as much as they did. Unlike their parents and grandparents, young people wouldn't wait patiently for new laws and court decisions. Instead, they were determined to end segregation immediately, through direct action. The four friends may have been surprised, however, by the show of support from their white peers. Three students from the University of North Carolina Women's College took stools at the lunch counter beside black protesters, making the sit-in an integrated movement.

> "[F]or the first time college kids saw that there was an opportunity where they could do something that could help a lot of people. Even help our parents."
>
> —Robert Tyrone Patterson, former A&T student, 1989

Gordon Blackwell, the chancellor of Women's College, wasn't pleased when newspapers across North Carolina reported that three of his students had joined the sit-in on Thursday. He warned the three women not to participate again. Although they promised to obey his request, Chancellor Blackwell decided to try and stop the protest. On Friday morning, while the sit-ins at Woolworth's and Kress continued, he called together administrators from other local colleges. After the meeting, these administrators immediately contacted Greensboro's

THE CONFEDERATE BATTLE FLAG:
SYMBOL OF PRIDE OR SYMBOL OF HATE?

During the Civil War, the red flag with a star-studded blue X was the symbol of the Confederate States of America, the new nation formed by Southerners who broke away from the United States. Southerners felt the U.S. government threatened their way of life, which at that time included slavery. As a result, the Civil War was fought over two key issues: states' rights and slavery. After the Union army defeated the Confederate army in 1865, the rebellious states joined the Union again. Southerners, however, did not give up the battle to protect states' rights and southern traditions. The flag of the Confederacy became the symbol of southern pride.

A century later, in the 1950s and 1960s, some southerners again thought the federal government threatened their way of life. This time the issue was segregation. When the U.S. Supreme Court called for the desegregation of public schools, some southerners fought back. They pulled out the Confederate flag as a symbol of states' rights and the long-standing system of segregation. Members of the Ku Klux Klan carried the flag in demonstration marches. Crowds in Little Rock, Arkansas, waved the flag when black teenagers tried to enter Central

business owners and student leaders. Someone suggested a moratorium on the sit-ins—similar to a cease-fire during a war to allow time for peace talks—so that negotiations could begin.

The A&T student representatives wouldn't agree to call off the sit-in without first consulting their fellow students. At a meeting on Saturday morning, the representatives proposed a two-week moratorium. Nearly fourteen hundred students voted unanimously against it. They were going to keep sitting until the stores gave black customers equal service.

High School. White students at the University of Alabama and the University of Mississippi paraded with the flag when their schools admitted African Americans. During the sit-in in Greensboro, protesters for desegregation held U.S. flags while their segregationist opponents clutched Confederate flags.

For southerners who supported black Americans' struggle for equality, the Confederate flag stood for things to be proud of—history, music, art, literature, and good manners. They scolded their neighbors for turning the flag into a symbol of everything to be ashamed of— segregation, prejudice, and racism. But the damage was done. For many blacks, the Confederate flag came to mean hate. In the twenty-first century, many years after the civil rights movement, the Confederate battle flag remains a controversial symbol.

The students went back downtown. Within hours their nonviolent protest came dangerously close to erupting in violence. February 6, 1960, in Greensboro would be remembered as Black Saturday.

When the A&T students and other protesters arrived in downtown Greensboro on Saturday morning, they faced a large gang of white youths. Black citizens and white citizens who had come to watch the excitement swelled the crowd. The A&T football players, who had joined the protest, entered Woolworth's. Carrying American flags and announcing they were the Union army, they cleared a path through the crowd to the lunch counter. As the protesters took seats, their opponents, waving Confederate flags, moved in. Tension grew with every passing minute.

As the outnumbered police officers wondered how long they could control the situation, a Woolworth's employee received a warning from an anonymous caller claiming a bomb was planted in the store. The employee alerted the officers, and they evacuated the building. The crowd at Woolworth's then converged on S. H. Kress, where the sit-ins had provoked a similarly explosive scene. Alarmed by the bomb scare at Woolworth's, the Kress manager decided not to take any risks. Leaping onto the lunch counter, he waved his arms, announced that the store was closed, and told everyone to go home.

Out on the street again, the student protesters shouted with triumph. Joyously, they marched in single file back to campus. That evening they voted for a moratorium while business owners, city leaders, and their own representatives negotiated the desegregation of downtown Greensboro.

THE SIT-INS SPREAD

Meanwhile, black students in other North Carolina cities launched sit-ins. On February 8—exactly one week after the four A&T freshmen demanded equal service at the Woolworth's store in Greensboro— student protesters occupied lunch counter stools in Winston-Salem and in Durham. On February 9, a group of students converged on the lunch counters in Charlotte. On February 10, another group targeted stores in

Male and female students in Little Rock, Arkansas, staged their own lunch counter sit-in at the Woolworth's store in that city in the early 1960s.

Raleigh. And the protests continued to spread. Within weeks, students in Virginia, South Carolina, Tennessee, Texas, Georgia, and Florida had joined the sit-in movement.

Despite rumors about a conspiracy, protesters in each city acted spontaneously and independently. Black students didn't need an outsider to stir their resentment of segregation, and they certainly didn't need anyone to give them orders. They had merely been waiting for inspiration. The Greensboro sit-in proved that young people had a role in the struggle for equality and gave them a new tactic—nonviolent protest.

The Greensboro sit-in wasn't actually the first. In 1958 NAACP Youth Councils in Oklahoma and Kansas had staged sit-ins at local stores. In 1959 members of another group, the Congress of Racial Equality (CORE), had held a sit-in at a lunch counter in Miami, Florida. Just months before the Greensboro protest, a sit-in took place in Durham, North Carolina. Around the same time, a group of students in Nashville, Tennessee, challenged segregation at downtown restaurants and lunch counters. Yet none of these protests had the same impact as the sit-in led by A&T students in February 1960.

What made the Greensboro sit-in different? The answer was simple. The press had ignored previous sit-ins. But newspapers, radio stations, and television newscasts across the United States reported the Greensboro sit-in. As the news spread, so did the movement. Ralph Johns, the businessman who encouraged McNeil and his friends to act, had recognized the importance of publicity. On the first day of the sit-in, he had called the news office of the Greensboro newspaper, the *Record*, to alert reporters that there was a story brewing at Woolworth's. Greensboro's city and student papers carried articles on the sit-in. Soon other papers in North Carolina began to cover the protest. Then on February 15, 1960, the *New York Times* brought the sit-in to national attention with a front-page headline: "Negro Sitdowns Stir Fear of Wider Unrest in South."

> **"Once the sit-ins started in Greensboro, [the movement] spread to practically every black city where there [was] a college in the state of North Carolina. It just kind of spread like a wildfire. It became contagious."**
>
> —Robert Tyrone Patterson, former A&T student, 1989

A long article by Claude Sitton appeared under that headline. Sitton was relatively new to the *New York Times*. He had worked as a staff journalist for less than two years. Some reporters considered anything happening outside New York and Washington, D.C., unworthy of notice, but Sitton took events in the South very seriously. He was the ideal person to cover southern news. Born in Georgia, Sitton attended Emory University in Atlanta before he became a reporter. He then worked for the International News Service and the United Press (later United Press International). He did a stint with the U.S. Information Agency before joining the New York Times as a copy editor in 1957. The next year, the Times made him a reporter and sent him south.

Sitton didn't wait for the news to come to him. When the student protests started in the winter of 1960, he traveled from city to city to report from the scenes of action. The Times published Sitton's first article on the sit-ins, written on location in Raleigh, North Carolina, on February 11. Four days later, the Times editors put his article, "Negro Sitdowns," on the front page.

Sitton opened the article by pointing out that sit-ins weren't mere student pranks. The protesters were serious, and they demanded more than a seat at the lunch counter. They demanded an end to segregation everywhere. Reporting the first day of the Greensboro sit-in, Sitton dramatized the scene at Woolworth's when the four A&T freshmen tried to order coffee. He then described confrontations between protesters and their opponents in other cities. Bullies insulted protesters, smashed eggs on them, and knocked them off the lunch counter stools. In South Carolina, someone tried to drive protesters out of a drugstore by throwing a bottle of ammonia, unleashing a cloud of choking fumes.

To give the Times reader a balanced perspective, Sitton quoted a number of different people. Some were black, some were white. Some supported the sit-ins, some did not. The list included a minister, a CORE representative, the mayor of Raleigh, the president of the Greensboro NAACP, and the North Carolina state attorney general.

For black youths who read Sitton's article, the quotations from McNeil and other student protesters had the most impact. Their words expressed common feelings. Their faces in newspaper photos and on television screens looked familiar. Many other black men and women felt encouraged to challenge segregation too. Inspired, they started protests in their own cities. As Sitton and his fellow reporters continued to cover the sit-ins throughout February and March 1960, the movement continued to spread.

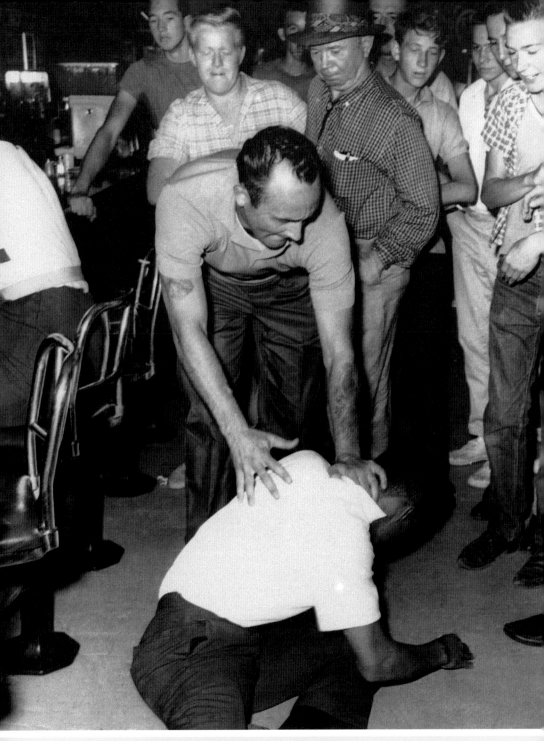

A sit-in participant is pulled from a stool and beaten at a Woolworth's lunch counter in Jackson, Mississippi, in 1963.

NEGOTIATIONS IN GREENSBORO

Greensboro's leaders ignored Claude Sitton's warning that protesters were serious in their demand for an end to segregation. Store owners seemed to believe they were the ones who scored a victory on Black Saturday because the students agreed to stop the sit-in. Facing no immediate threat to their profits, downtown business owners saw no reason to change their segregation policies.

One man who did take the students seriously was Edward R. Zane. When Mayor George Roach had sought advice on how to handle the sit-in, Zane offered to help. A member of the city council and an executive at Burlington Industries, Zane had contact with both city officials and businesspeople. He also knew key leaders in Greensboro's African American community. By bringing these groups together, he believed he could work out an agreement. Before he could open negotiations, the sit-in had erupted into the Black Saturday confrontation. When the students voted for a two-week moratorium, Zane seized the opportunity to find a peaceful solution.

> "It's not a case of black and white. It's a case of law, justice. I'm not fighting for the person because he's black or because he's yellow. I'm fighting for the reason that any form of segregation, any method of denying to a citizen equal rights . . . can only hurt the nation."
>
> —Edward R. Zane, Greensboro business leader and member of city council, in 1987 interview

First, Zane met with student leaders at the Hayes-Taylor YMCA. As a white city councilman and business executive, he represented the political and economic forces that had oppressed African Americans for centuries—the very forces the students were resisting. Yet as a human being, he shared the students' outrage against injustice, discrimination, and segregation. He believed all Americans deserved the same rights. During the meeting at the YMCA, he praised the protesters for their courage and self-discipline. By convincing the students of his commitment to equality and treating them with respect, Zane won their trust.

Zane also made clear, however, that he didn't approve of protest tactics. A graduate of Georgetown University Law School in Washington, D.C., he had faith in the law and the political system. Although the sit-in was nonviolent, he said that it violated store owners' property rights. Instead of generating sympathy, the sit-in sparked fear and hostility. For this reason, Zane urged the students to negotiate. He proposed a special committee of business and city leaders to study segregation in downtown Greensboro. While the committee tried to reach a settlement, students had to stay away from the lunch counters. A sit-in at this critical moment could backfire.

Edward R. Zane *(shown here in the 1980s)* **was on the Greensboro City Council during the sit-ins. He helped negotiate a final settlement between the student protesters and Greensboro businesses owners.**

The students agreed to Zane's proposal. On February 21, the *Daily News* approvingly reported their willingness to negotiate. In response, Mayor Roach appointed a committee to work out a solution and named Zane the chairman.

As Zane started settlement talks with business leaders, he also conducted a mail survey of public opinion. Woolworth's executives claimed they had no nationwide company policy regarding segregation. The manager of each store was instructed to follow local customs. Stores in the South ran segregated lunch counters because, managers claimed, white customers refused to dine with black customers. To convince Woolworth's manager C. L. Harris to desegregate the lunch counter, therefore, Zane believed he had to prove the public favored desegregation. At the same time, as a native of Tennessee, Zane recognized the force of Jim Crow taboos. He wondered if the citizens of Greensboro were truly ready for whites and blacks to sit side by side at public eating places.

More than two thousand citizens responded to Zane's public opinion survey. The majority (73 percent) said businesses should give blacks and whites equal service. The editors of the *Daily News* also called for equality. Yet Greensboro's citizens didn't vote unanimously in favor of desegregation—27 percent voted against it. These were the customers Harris and his fellow managers seemed most concerned about.

Despite a shared fear of alienating white customers, business leaders disagreed about how to address the question of desegregation. On the one hand, some reasoned that since student protesters had held sit-ins only at Woolworth's and S. H. Kress, only the managers of these two stores had to deal with the problem. The managers of Woolworth's and Kress, on the other hand, felt they had been singled out unfairly. If they had to desegregate, they argued, every downtown store and restaurant should have to desegregate. Negotiations dragged on. It seemed as though business and city leaders were deliberately stalling, hoping students would lose interest in the sit-in.

"It was not an isolated case of getting one institution to open the counters; we wanted the whole community to respond."

—Joseph McNeil, 1979

Zane, however, remembered his promise to the students. On March 24, 1960, in one last effort to reach a resolution, he met with store managers. They had rejected his recommendation that they let every customer, regardless of skin color, sit at the lunch counters. They had rejected his proposal to remove the stools and make every customer stand. They had rejected his suggestion that they close the lunch counters. This time they rejected his plan for divided lunch counters, with one section reserved for white customers and one desegregated section. Zane's efforts to negotiate had failed.

"We didn't do it [start the sit-in] for personal recognition or anything like that."

—Ezell Blair Jr., 1979

RETURN TO THE LUNCH COUNTER

Since the evening of February 6, when the students agreed to a moratorium, they had kept their word and stayed away from the lunch counters. They made clear, though, that they had not changed their minds about demanding equal service. On March 26, the New York Times carried two articles on the situation in Greensboro. The first profiled Junior Blair. The anonymous journalist who wrote the article discussed the connection between the sit-in and Mohandas Gandhi's nonviolent protests in India. Like Gandhi, Blair was prepared to go to jail for his peaceful activism. The journalist portrayed Blair as a considerate, well-mannered young man. Under a photograph of Blair wearing a suit jacket and a bow tie, he was quoted as saying he tried to see the other person's perspective.

In the second article, another journalist described the sit-in that had taken place in early February and the efforts of the committee studying segregation since then. Blair was quoted as saying he had confidence in the committee. The students were getting impatient, however. If downtown stores refused to desegregate, Blair warned, protesters would return to the lunch counters.

Once again, Greensboro's leaders ignored a warning. On March 31, Zane sadly announced to the students that the committee was deadlocked. Negotiations had failed. For Blair and his peers, the tactics of nonviolent protest seemed the only option left. The next day, they returned to the lunch counters, determined to continue the sit-ins until they won equality.

CHAPTER 6

SUPPORTERS AND **OPPONENTS**

"[The sit-in] was really a community effort in the true sense of the word."

—Joseph McNeil, 1979

On April 1, 1960, exactly two months after Junior Blair and his friends launched the first sit-in, a second outbreak of protests struck downtown Greensboro. As students from A&T College and Bennett College began picketing, C. L. Harris closed the lunch counter at Woolworth's. His supervisors at company headquarters in Atlanta, Georgia, had advised him that temporarily closing one area of the store was better than facing another sit-in. Down the street, the Kress store adopted a different strategy. When forty-five blacks occupied the lunch counter, the manager had them arrested.

The manager of the Kress store in Greensboro had sit-in protesters at his lunch counter arrested. Hundreds of local citizens supported the students with a demonstration outside the store.

When Harris closed the lunch counter at Woolworth's in Greensboro, protesters picketed outside the store.

The arrests didn't end the protests. On the contrary, students became even more determined. The entire black community rallied behind them. During the spring and summer of 1960, this pattern—resistance to protesters followed by an overwhelming wave of support—appeared in city after city. As reporters spread the news across the United States about courageous black students challenging segregation, young people and adults, blacks and whites, northerners and southerners, local civic groups and national organizations joined the struggle for equality. Nonviolent protest, these supporters believed, would conquer the fear, hatred, and brutality of their opponents. Although Greensboro's citizens focused on events in their own city, they knew they were taking part in a national movement.

RALLYING GREENSBORO'S BLACK CITIZENS

Nell Coley, an English teacher at Dudley High School, had always tried to instill pride and self-confidence in her students. When she heard about the sit-in initiated by two former Dudley students, Junior Blair and David Richmond, she went downtown to see for herself. The sight of young blacks politely demanding equal service at the lunch counters thrilled her. She shared the student protesters' triumphant joy on Black Saturday when Woolworth's and Kress were forced to close.

During the first week of the sit-in, several key figures in the black community also showed support. Dr. George Simkins, head of the Greensboro NAACP, had tried for years to end segregation at Cone Memorial Hospital, city schools, the public golf course, and other public places. Naturally, he sympathized with the students. Fellow NAACP members did too. On the second day of the sit-in, they agreed to provide assistance if it was needed. One NAACP member, the minister Otis Hairston, offered the students use of the mimeograph machine at Shiloh Baptist Church for copying fliers about their protest. Perhaps Hairston felt an obligation to help because two of the four who had started the sit-in attended his church.

President Warmoth Gibbs and Dean William Gamble of A&T College supported the sit-in indirectly by refusing to intervene. Gibbs and Gamble cooperated with Gordon Blackwell, chancellor of the University of North Carolina's Women's College, in arranging negotiations between student leaders and Greensboro business owners. Yet in contrast to Blackwell, the A&T administrators did not scold students for protesting. Gamble ignored Mayor George Roach's plea that the college

Warmoth Gibbs (shown here in the 1980s) was president of A&T at the time of the sit-ins. He quietly supported the movement.

discipline students. Gibbs asserted that what students did on their own time was their own business. He wouldn't send them to their dorm rooms for protesting segregation.

As the sit-in movement spread throughout North Carolina in February and March, state officials put increasing pressure on college administrators. Governor Luther Hodges wrote to college presidents, urging them to halt the protests. In addition, ignoring the students' commitment to nonviolence, he publicly declared the protests a danger to society. Malcolm Seawell, state attorney general, pronounced the sit-ins illegal. A lunch counter was the store owner's private property, he reasoned. The protesters should be arrested for trespassing.

These announcements from the highest state officials were a serious matter for A&T administrators. As a public institution, A&T depended on the state government for funding. If state officials decided to cut funding until the protests ended, Gibbs and Gamble wouldn't be able to pay professors' salaries or buy food for the dining hall. Despite these concerns, Gibbs and Gamble stood firm. They refused to punish the student protesters or try to stop the sit-ins.

Willa Player, president of Bennett College, also refused to let financial concerns override her support for the students. In mid-February, she received a letter from Spencer Love, the owner of Burlington Industries and one of Greensboro's wealthiest men. He was also a segregationist who would not hire African American workers at his textile factories. Nonetheless, Love considered himself a benefactor of the black community because, among other projects, he had made a donation to build an indoor swimming pool at the Hayes-Taylor YMCA. When the sit-in began, he clearly thought black leaders should listen to his advice.

In his letter, Love assured Player that he was in favor of progress. But progress took time, and young people were much too impatient. Without ordering Player to stop the sit-in, Love implied that she should control the Bennett students. When Player answered this letter, she didn't think about future donations. In frank but polite words, she wrote that she hoped Love would speak to Mayor Roach about the need for all citizens to work together for equality.

Simkins, Hairston, Gibbs, and Player each took a risk in supporting the students. Other adults were more reluctant to take sides. If a man joined the sit-in, he might be arrested or lose his job. Angry citizens might beat him, terrorize his family, or burn down his house. Junior Blair and Joe McNeil acknowledged that college students could afford to speak out against segregation because they didn't have full-time jobs or families. These two protest leaders understood why many adults were afraid to help.

> **"Although in this movement there were various factions [groups] in opposition as to what we thought the goal was, or how fast we should achieve our goal, we were fortunate in Greensboro to have people on both sides who were learned people and who knew how to conduct themselves in a manner which brought this thing out for the better of everybody. . . . But we did learn a lot . . . everybody could hug and kiss and say, 'Hey, we're still friends.'"**
>
> —Ezell Blair Jr., 1979

At the same time, students needed the support of the entire black community. When negotiations failed and the protest resumed on April 1, 1960, students added another nonviolent tactic: a boycott. Everyone from college presidents to janitors, from grandmothers to teenagers could join a boycott. It didn't take time away from work or school. It didn't violate the law. Best of all, a boycott was highly effective. Appealing to a store manager's conscience might not work, but appealing to his business sense certainly would. If blacks, who accounted for 25 percent of Greensboro's population, refused to shop at a store with a segregated lunch counter, profits would drop.

Black churches, the local NAACP, the Greensboro Men's Club, the Greensboro Citizens Association, and other organizations spread the news about the boycott. The response was amazing. Player turned in her credit card at Meyer's because the department store had a segregated dining room. Black business owners offered bail money if protesters were arrested. High school students volunteered to picket. College students welcomed assistance but refused to give up leadership of the movement they had started.

NATIONWIDE SUPPORT

As the weeks passed, the boycott took a toll on downtown businesses. At Woolworth's, Harris watched sales fall by thousands of dollars. But the Greensboro store wasn't the only Woolworth's store losing sales. Stores across the South had already been hit by the outbreak of sit-ins.

As Americans who believed in equality joined a nationwide boycott, the entire company was struck. Some protesters even picketed at the Woolworth's stores in New York City, although the company served African Americans at lunch counters in northern cities.

News reporters who spread the word about the sit-ins and the boycott were the student protesters' most influential allies. *New York Times* reporter Claude Sitton covered the sit-ins from Raleigh, North Carolina, to Montgomery, Alabama. Throughout the spring and summer of 1960, the *Times* also carried frequent updates from Atlanta, Georgia, where one of the largest student protests had begun in mid-March. Meanwhile, reporter David Halberstam provided ongoing coverage

Reporter David Halberstam covered the sit-ins and protests in Nashville, Tennessee. He went on to win a Pulitzer Prize in 1964 for his coverage of the Vietnam War (1957–1975).

of the protests in Nashville, Tennessee. His articles appeared in the newspaper *The Tennessean* and in the national newsmagazine *The Reporter*.

Officially, reporters weren't supposed to take sides. They were supposed to present the news in a neutral way. By treating the sit-ins as important events, however, reporters brought them to the attention

> "The sit-ins would not have been successful had it not been for the coverage and presence of national radio, television, and newspapers."
>
> —*Ralph Johns, Greensboro businessman, 1979*

of every American who read the newspaper, listened to the radio, or watched television. Reporters often selected photos and motion pictures of sit-ins across the South that evoked sympathy for the protesters. Americans saw neatly dressed students sitting at an empty lunch counter, tough-looking teens pressing lighted cigarettes against the backs of young women, protesters with sugar in their hair and ketchup smeared on their clothes, and police officers packing students into police vans.

Protesters in Harlem—an African American neighborhood in New York City—picket outside a Woolworth's to support the sit-ins in the South. Most Woolworth's lunch counters in the North were not segregated.

Reporters pointed out that many of the protesters were white. News photos picturing white students carrying picket signs and sitting at lunch counters side by side with black students proved whites had joined the movement. These photos enabled white Americans to imagine themselves as protesters and inspired them to picket or support the boycott.

Students quickly recognized that such favorable publicity was their key to success. Nashville students, for example, kept Halberstam informed of their plans because they wanted a reporter on the scene. Halberstam

> "I remember my whole family were all sitting looking
> at television when we saw [news about the sit-in]
> and there was like this exhilaration. . . . In some sense
> you project yourself into it. . . . You identify with this
> courageous and creative thing that people are doing
> and it's liberating. It really was a liberating feeling."
>
> —*The Reverend Nelson Napoleon Johnson, Littleton, North Carolina, 1989*

welcomed this inside information because it was his job to stay on top of the action. Personally, he believed segregation was wrong. He was twenty-five years old in 1960, and he felt a bond with the young protesters. Reporting their campaign to the nation was his way of helping them. By making Americans aware of discrimination against African Americans in the South and the violence used to suppress protest, Halberstam, Sitton, and other reporters assisted in the struggle for equality.

National leaders of the NAACP, who considered themselves the frontline fighters in the struggle for equality, initially refused to endorse the sit-ins. Committed to legal and political tactics, these men and women feared that protest—even nonviolent protest—would backfire. They feared that, instead of ending segregation, prejudiced white citizens might try even harder to keep blacks out of schools, parks, hospitals, restaurants, offices, and factories. As the sit-ins spread, however, the NAACP's national leaders realized that if they didn't support the movement, they'd be left behind. Some local chapters, such as the Greensboro NAACP, were collaborating with student protesters.

Other civil rights organizations were lending a hand as well. The Congress of Racial Equality, a group created for nonviolent protest, had sent a representative to North Carolina during the first week of the sit-ins. Soon CORE workers joined the movement in other states too.

Martin Luther King Jr., founder of the Southern Christian Leadership Conference (SCLC), had declared his support a few weeks after the protests began.

▊ ▊ ▊ THE OPPONENTS

In many southern cities, the protesters were treated as criminals. Some city officials thought they could put an end to the sit-in movement simply by arresting protesters. Other officials were more willing to negotiate, but they wanted to appear in control of the situation.

Officials justified arrests by claiming sit-ins, marches, and pickets threatened law and order because they blocked traffic and disrupted business. They claimed protesters were a threat to public safety because confrontations between protesters and opponents could instantly break into violence. On Black Saturday, for example, the crowd in downtown Greensboro could have turned into a rioting mob. If there really had been a bomb planted at Woolworth's, as the anonymous caller alleged, it could have killed thousands of people. Pointing to such risks, southern city officials frequently charged protesters with disorderly conduct.

Another common charge against protesters was trespassing. City officials cited North Carolina attorney general Malcolm Seawell's

Lunch counters throughout the South closed in the early 1960s rather than serve African Americans.

pronouncement that a lunch counter was private property. It belonged to the store owner, who had the right to serve—or refuse to serve—whomever he or she wanted. According to this logic, a sit-in violated the store owner's property rights. Some thought a businessperson's property rights mattered more than black citizens' civil rights.

President Dwight D. Eisenhower would not say whose rights should take priority. During a press conference on March 16, 1960, a reporter asked about the protests sweeping the southern states. Eisenhower responded that Americans could protest in a legal way to win their constitutional rights. But then he immediately stepped back from his own statement. He claimed that since he wasn't a lawyer, he didn't

EISENHOWER COMMENTS ON THE SIT-INS

During a news conference on March 16, 1960, President Dwight D. Eisenhower expressed his views on the sit-ins. As with school desegregation, he refused to take a strong stand. He stressed that, unlike voting rights—which the federal government had a responsibility to protect—segregation was a local issue that each community had to deal with on its own. He didn't support the federal government intervening in local affairs. Eisenhower made it clear, however, that nonviolent protest was an American tradition.

President Dwight D. Eisenhower in 1960

know what kinds of protests were legal. A few minutes later, he noted that while segregation in public institutions was unconstitutional, the U.S. Supreme Court had to decide if segregation in other places violated black citizens' constitutional rights. He also said that, in his opinion, the government interfered too much in Americans' private affairs.

Although Eisenhower didn't condemn the protesters, he didn't support them either. He deliberately left open questions about the legitimacy of their tactics and what places counted as private property. The protesters' opponents could interpret Eisenhower's cautious comments as approval of segregated lunch counters.

City officials believed they had all the justification they needed to stop the sit-in movement—and they would do so by force, if necessary. When students in Nashville, Atlanta, and Greensboro were arrested, their calm, peaceful manner surprised police. Later in court, their decision to serve jail time instead of paying bail shocked judges. Clearly the prospect of going to jail didn't deter these young protesters.

This woman was arrested during a sit-in in Raleigh, North Carolina, in April 1960.

The prospect of jail disturbed many older leaders of the struggle for equality, however. Although the NAACP encouraged the boycotts and provided legal assistance, it continued to question the students' protest tactics. Thurgood Marshall, the NAACP lawyer who had helped defeat school segregation in *Brown v. Board of Education*, demonstrated this ambivalent encouragement. On April 3, 1960, Marshall gave a talk at Bennett College in Greensboro. He urged students not to settle for token desegregation but to keep fighting until they won full equality. That same month, Marshall advised students that, if they were arrested, they should get out of jail on bail as quickly as possible.

Marshall may have meant well, but students resented this advice. For them, the "jail-in" was an exciting new form of protest. Their inspiration, Mohandas Gandhi, had gone to prison several times, and Martin Luther King Jr. called on protesters to fill the jails. Hundreds of students chose to go to jail rather than pay bail when they were arrested. They believed the sight of innocent young men and women behind bars would awaken Americans' conscience. On another level, jail was a test of a person's commitment to the struggle. Whoever passed the test earned a badge of courage.

In Orangeburg, South Carolina, officials tried a different strategy. During a mass demonstration in mid-March 1960, police bombed students with tear gas, sprayed them with water hoses, and hauled them to jail. When

Kress store officials removed the seats of the lunch counter stools at this store in Orangeburg, South Carolina, in 1960 so that no one could sit down.

Police stand outside a pen of protesters in Orangeburg, South Carolina. After the city jails were full, police herded protesters into this outdoor stockade.

there was no more room in the jail, police crowded the wet, gagging students into an outdoor pen.

In addition to brutal police, protesters faced angry white citizens who called them names, spat on them, threw food at them, and burned them with cigarettes. Sometimes opponents used more violent tactics. In Montgomery, Alabama, mobs attacked protesters. The police did little to stop the beatings, and the violence eventually became so bad that protesters called off the sit-ins.

The Ku Klux Klan was often blamed for attacks on protesters. But KKK members weren't the only citizens who resisted desegregation. Some respectable white citizens claimed desegregation violated their own freedom, their freedom of choice. They insisted that white Americans had the right to choose whom they would ride with on the bus or sit beside at a lunch counter. The manager of the Woolworth's store in Greensboro agreed with this way of thinking. By resisting desegregation, Harris believed he was defending the rights of his white customers who wanted to eat only with persons like themselves.

A black student pickets outside the Woolworth's in Greensboro in 1960, while a counter-protester keeps step with him carrying his own hostile sign.

A number of southerners were honestly uncomfortable with sitting down beside an African American person. For decades, the Jim Crow customs of the South had kept blacks and whites separate. Men and women who had grown up with those customs may have agreed that all Americans had a right to equality, but they could not change their own habits overnight.

■ A CONSPIRACY THEORY

Even some southerners who thought they got along well with African Americans felt threatened by the sit-in movement. They'd never realized African Americans resented segregation because few dared to complain about it. Suddenly, protesters were demanding an end to it. Refusing to believe that local blacks had started the protests by themselves, some white citizens blamed outsiders for stirring up trouble. When former president Harry S. Truman suggested that Communists were behind the sit-ins, however, an editorial writer in the *New York Times* pointed out that Truman had no evidence to prove a conspiracy existed.

Most Americans probably agreed with the editorial writer: the conspiracy theory was just plain silly. And yet they couldn't understand how four college freshmen in Greensboro had started a nationwide protest movement. The students must have made some sort of plan. Some sort of organization must be in charge.

In fact, Junior Blair and his three friends had no master plan before they sat down at the Woolworth's lunch counter on February 1, 1960. As news about the Greensboro sit-in spread, students across the South spontaneously started their own sit-ins. Students soon realized, though, that they could learn from and help each other. In mid-April 1960, they gathered at a university in North Carolina to unite forces.

"A lot of people saw negotiating as submission. . . . Yes, there was a prize to be won, but we weren't going to win it by just eliminating the enemy. We wanted to convert the enemy more than anything else."

—Franklin McCain, 1979

CHAPTER 7

UNITING
FORCES

Success to us was whatever good comes to the movement, because of the movement. And success wasn't a personal thing. I think that's probably one key to the success of the movement, that we didn't equate success as being personal."

—Franklin McCain, 1979

Junior Blair was an expert on sit-ins. He knew how to schedule protesters in shifts so that the counter stools would always be filled, yet no one would miss a class. He knew how to respond to store employees and how to recruit supporters. If asked for advice, he could give suggestions for everything from dressing for a sit-in to negotiating with city leaders.

Meanwhile, student protesters in other cities were learning to organize sit-ins on their own. They were also testing a variety of other strategies—boycotts, picket lines, demonstration marches, and jail-ins. These students had tips for making waterproof signs, guidelines for peacefully responding to violence, and advice for answering the judge properly in court. For the sit-in movement to succeed, students across the United States needed to share with each other what they had learned. They needed to coordinate the protests in each town and city to launch a nationwide campaign against segregation.

The one person who saw the potential of an organized student protest movement was a middle-aged black woman, Ella Baker. Baker had joined the struggle for equality as a graduate student in the 1930s. During the 1940s, she served as a field secretary for the

BIGGER THAN A HAMBURGER

A middle-aged woman dressed in a long skirt and a jacket, Ella Baker must have reminded the students at the 1960 protest movement conference in Raleigh, North Carolina, of a schoolteacher. Yet, she understood their feelings—their excitement and their fear—because she too had joined the struggle for equality as a young person. In her speech, Baker reminded the students that the sit-in movement wasn't about sodas and hamburgers. The real goal was to end segregation and discrimination everywhere so that blacks could enjoy their full rights as Americans.

Ella Baker *(left)* organized a conference at Shaw University in Raleigh, North Carolina, to bring protesting students together to learn from each other. Here she speaks at a news conference in the late 1960s.

NAACP. In 1958 she went to work for the Southern Christian Leadership Conference. When the sit-ins began in early 1960, she was the SCLC's executive director, working at the association's headquarters in Atlanta, Georgia, with Martin Luther King Jr.

Inspired by the students' bold courage, Baker wanted to help them, although she also wanted them to remain independent. They had started the sit-in movement, so she believed they shouldn't surrender control to the NAACP or the SCLC. The answer, she decided, was to give them the opportunity to create an organization of their own.

The first step was bringing students together. Baker sent letters to colleges throughout the South, inviting protest leaders to a weekend conference at Shaw University in Raleigh, North Carolina. More than one hundred twenty black students and a dozen white students from fifty-six southern colleges and high schools attended the conference. Junior Blair and Billy Smith went to Raleigh as representatives of A&T College. They had read newspaper reports about the sit-ins in other cities. The conference gave the two representatives from Greensboro the opportunity to meet the individuals behind the headlines.

GATHERING IN RALEIGH

For three days, from April 15 until April 17, 1960, Blair and Smith exchanged ideas and swapped stories with fellow protesters. Smith talked about training high school students to carry on the protest when college students went home over the summer break. He also described a plan to knock on doors in Greensboro's black neighborhoods and ask residents to boycott segregated stores. Harold Bardonille, a student at South Carolina State College in Orangeburg, described the day the Orangeburg police attacked protesters with water hoses. When a group of black farmers heard the news, they came to the college to offer support. For those who attended the conference, Bardonille's story proved that adults were looking to young people for leadership.

During the conference, students held workshops to discuss important topics. In one workshop, they studied the philosophy of nonviolence. In another, they resolved that college administrators should not expel a student for protesting. At the workshop "Jail vs. Bail," participants encouraged anyone who was arrested to serve a prison sentence rather than pay bail. Those who attended the session on integration within the protest movement itself concluded that blacks and whites should work together. These workshops gave students the opportunity to find solutions to specific problems.

Recognizing that the sit-ins were part of a greater struggle for equality, students willingly listened to experienced civil rights leaders who spoke at the conference. In his speech on protest tactics, Martin Luther King Jr. recommended a nationwide boycott of segregated stores. Instead of the word *boycott*, however, he used the more friendly term *selective buying*. He also urged protesters not to pay bail if they were arrested.

Martin Luther King Jr. spoke at the conference for student protest leaders at North Carolina's Shaw University in April 1960. He recommended that arrested students should stay in jail to gain publicity for their cause.

News photos of innocent persons in prison, he thought, would make Americans see the injustice of segregation. Finally, urging students to examine the philosophy of nonviolence, King announced that their true goal was a community held together by love.

James Lawson, another speaker at the conference, was a well-known expert on nonviolence. For him, it was not merely a protest tactic; it was a way of life. In the early 1950s, Lawson had refused to register for the military draft because he believed war was wrong. Rather than kill anyone—even an enemy soldier—Lawson chose to go to prison. When he was freed in 1953, he went to India. There he had the opportunity to study Mohandas Gandhi's philosophy of nonviolence in Gandhi's own country.

During the civil rights movement of the 1950s and 1960s, Martin Luther King Jr. emerged as a champion of nonviolent protest. Born in 1929, King grew up in Atlanta, Georgia, where he experienced racial discrimination. He didn't become actively involved in the struggle for equality as a student. Then, in 1955, while he was serving as the minister of a Baptist church in Montgomery, Alabama, he agreed to lead a boycott of segregated buses. As a result of this experience, King discovered his calling as a leader of the civil rights movement.

Following Gandhi's example, King insisted upon the use of nonviolent tactics to end segregation and to win voting rights. But King didn't just stand behind his pulpit and issue orders. He joined sit-ins, walked in marches, spoke at rallies, and served time in jail. Although he didn't always achieve specific goals, his campaign for civil rights succeeded in making the world aware that the United States denied African Americans equality.

In April 1968, during a protest in Memphis, Tennessee, King was assassinated. Every January, Americans honor him on the national holiday devoted to his memory, Martin Luther King Day.

Lawson did not stay in India long. When he heard about the rising struggle for equality back home, he returned to the United States and volunteered his help. Working for the Fellowship of Reconciliation (FOR), a national civil rights organization, he traveled around the South and taught workshops on nonviolence. In 1958 Lawson enrolled in Vanderbilt University Divinity School in Nashville, Tennessee, although he continued to run workshops on nonviolence.

Soon a handful of students from local colleges began to attend Lawson's workshops. He encouraged the students to share their feelings about segregation and led group discussions about facing discrimination with dignity. He also trained the students for nonviolent protest. During practice sessions, some played the role of protesters. Others, in the role of opponents, called the protesters names and shoved and slapped them.

The discussions and training sessions had a strong influence on the students, but Lawson's personal example had even more impact. Once, when a man spat on him in public, Lawson quietly asked for the man's handkerchief. The man was so surprised he simply gave it to Lawson. After Lawson dried off the spit and returned the handkerchief, he started talking with the man about motorcycles. In this way, Lawson turned an angry

The Reverend James Lawson was a well-known speaker on nonviolent protests. He spoke to the students at the Shaw University conference in April 1960.

confrontation into a polite conversation and proved a person really could win by choosing nonviolence. Lawson had another opportunity to set an example when the sit-ins spread to Nashville in February 1960 and participants in his workshop took charge of the movement. Administrators at the divinity school accused him of stirring up the protesters and expelled him. Although he was only a few months away from graduation, he didn't fight back.

When Lawson spoke at the conference in Raleigh, he made clear that the unfair treatment he had received was not the issue behind the protests. The real issue, he said, was the "moral issue"—the moral evil of racism. As a minister, Lawson blended the philosophy of nonviolence with Christian ideas. Segregation was a sin because God did not discriminate against anyone. Christians had to fight back with love for all human beings. Nonviolent protest was both a judgment and a promise, Lawson declared. It was a judgment against the sin of hate and a promise to build a new society.

Just as Lawson urged the students to think about the moral issue, Ella Baker reminded them that the right to order a hamburger at a lunch counter was only a tiny step toward a much larger goal. That goal was equality, and Baker urged students to practice equality in their own lives. Over the years, she had seen how leaders could become greedy for fame and power. She hoped that, rather than join a leader-centered group, the students would form an organization of their own with group-centered leadership.

King, apparently, expected the students to create a youth group within his organization, the SCLC. But the students rejected this plan. They also refused to join FOR or CORE, both of which had sent representatives to the conference. Students were impatient with older leaders who seemed afraid to take action and whose tactics seemed outdated. The time had come for younger leaders and the new tactics of nonviolent protest. Students also decided against joining other young people's organizations that had sent representatives to Raleigh.

On the final day of the conference, the students created an organization of their own. They called it the Student Nonviolent Coordinating Committee. The name was a mouthful, so they quickly shortened it to SNCC, pronounced as one word: "Snick." Marion Barry, a student at Fisk University in Nashville, was elected SNCC's first chairman. The students also voted to adopt a statement of purpose. Written by Lawson, the statement repeated the message of his speech at the conference. Nonviolence, the statement declared, was SNCC's guiding principle because the power of love would overcome evil. Through nonviolence, SNCC aimed to build a society with justice for all citizens.

The founding of SNCC marked an important step in the student protest movement that had begun on February 1, 1960, when Blair and his friends sat down at the Woolworth's lunch counter. Inspired by these four freshmen, students across the South had immediately launched sit-ins in their own cities. Yet before Baker brought the sit-in leaders together in Raleigh in mid-April, each group had acted independently. Just as she had hoped, the conference gave student protesters the opportunity to get to know one another. As they discussed common problems, they realized how much they could learn from each other. They also realized how powerful the protest movement could become if, instead of working separately, they united forces.

There was no time during the conference to decide how the new organization would operate or what role it would play. For the young men and women in the protest movement, creating SNCC was like making a pact—a pact to meet again and to share information. In the same way, adopting a statement of purpose was like taking a vow—a vow of commitment to nonviolence.

▨ ▨ ▨ ▨ AN EXPLOSION IN NASHVILLE

On April 19, 1960, only two days after the conference, protesters in Nashville faced a critical test of their commitment to nonviolence. That morning, opponents of desegregation set off a bomb at the home of Z. Alexander Looby, a black lawyer. The explosion destroyed the house and broke windows in the medical school across the street. However, Looby and his wife escaped with only minor injuries. Black citizens saw the bomb as a direct attack against themselves because Looby

The students who joined SNCC set an example for cooperation among blacks and whites. In many southern counties, African Americans encountered discrimination and, sometimes, violence if they tried to vote. For this reason, in the summer of 1964, SNCC organized a campaign to encourage African Americans to register to vote. Black students and white students from the North and South volunteered for this risky mission. Together, they faced threats, beatings, and arrests. The SNCC Freedom Summer campaign made discrimination against black voters national news and helped to convince Congress to pass the Voting Rights Act of 1965.

Two volunteers with the SNCC Freedom Summer campaign talk to a potential voter in Mississippi in August 1964.

had led the struggle for equality in Nashville for years. He worked for the NAACP and served on the city council. A few weeks earlier, when students were arrested during a sit-in, he had represented them in court.

Emergency crews and onlookers stand outside the home *(above)* of Z. Alexander Looby *(below)*, an activist lawyer, after his home was bombed on April 19, 1960.

Nashville's black students were especially disturbed by the bombing. They wondered how they should respond to the attack and how to force Nashville's business and city leaders to admit that segregation was wrong. The students found an answer: a peaceful mass march. About noon on April 19, students from Tennessee Agricultural and Industrial College began walking toward city hall. Soon students from Fisk University and teenagers from Pearl High School fell in step with them. The crowd grew to four thousand as more and more citizens—youths and adults, blacks and whites—joined the march. Mayor Ben West went out to meet them on the steps of city hall.

A minister spoke first. He blamed the mayor for the bombing and demanded an end to segregation. White citizens, the minister declared, could no longer deny the rights of black citizens. After this angry outburst, a young woman named Diane Nash stepped forward.

Nash, a student at Fisk University, was a regular participant in Lawson's workshops on nonviolence. Those workshops, combined with her recent experience as a leader of the sit-ins, gave her self-confidence. Nash calmly asked Mayor West if he thought discrimination was wrong. He had to admit that, personally, he believed it was wrong. Then he agreed to set up a committee with both black and white members to work for the desegregation of downtown stores.

Nash and her fellow protesters in Nashville passed the test and set an example of nonviolence in action. They also proved that nonviolence was a powerful tactic. On May 10, 1960, six lunch counters and four

Anti-segregation protester Diane Nash *(second from left)* discusses civil rights at a meeting of the Republican Party in Chicago, Illinois, in 1960.

theaters in Nashville gave blacks equal service. When the owners of other stores, restaurants, and theaters saw that desegregation was good for business, they agreed to give black customers equal service too.

■ ■ ■ ■ CONTINUING THE STRUGGLE IN GREENSBORO

While the Nashville protesters celebrated a victory, students in Greensboro continued their own struggle against segregation. The negotiations that began in February dragged on for nearly two months. When they proved fruitless, the students began protesting again on April 1. After Woolworth's and Kress closed their lunch counters to prevent sit-ins, students picketed the stores.

And still store managers refused to desegregate. Perhaps they thought that picketing was a passing fad. Or maybe they thought that the protest leaders were seniors who would leave town after graduation in May and that life in Greensboro would return to normal. At the very least, store managers must have hoped for a few months of relief when the college students went home for the summer.

Businesspeople who held such hopes underestimated the protesters' dedication and the power of nonviolent tactics. African Americans had been struggling to win equality for more than one hundred years. College students knew they couldn't end segregation overnight. When they held a sit-in, they sent a message as clear as spoken words: we demand equality, and we're not leaving until we get it. To keep the protest going during the summer break, they trained high school volunteers to picket. College students also enlisted adults for a boycott of Woolworth's and other businesses that practiced segregation.

May passed, then June. Picketers continued to parade on the sidewalks. Customers continued to boycott targeted stores. On the surface, it appeared the protesters had reached a brick wall. Gradually, though, the picket lines and the boycott wore down the businesspeople's resistance to desegregation. Watching his profits drop, Woolworth's manager C. L. Harris decided he was ready to negotiate. The manager of Kress and the manager of Meyer's Department Store were ready too. In July, all three agreed to open their lunch counters to African American customers.

As negotiations between business owners and protesters dragged on,
protesters continued to march outside the Woolworth's in Greensboro.

Harris thought he had no choice, but he saw desegregation as a risky experiment. What would he do if white customers suddenly refused to shop at Woolworth's? He wanted to make desegregation seem as natural as possible so they would be comfortable. He requested that, instead of crowding the lunch counter on the first day, black customers come to Woolworth's a few at a time.

On July 25, 1960, the Woolworth's waitress served the first African Americans sitting at the lunch counter. These diners were not actually customers but store employees. Apparently, Harris worried about losing control of the situation and thought he could rely on his own employees to prevent trouble. Such worries were unnecessary. There was no trouble. Over the next few days, three hundred African Americans ate at Woolworth's. Black customers were polite; and white customers didn't complain, at least not publicly. By the time the college

This lunch counter in Texas was integrated in 1960.

students returned for the fall semester, a black person sitting down at a lunch counter was an everyday occurrence in Greensboro.

Every individual who participated in the sit-ins, pickets, and boycotts helped to win equal service for African Americans at the lunch counters in downtown Greensboro. Students—especially Junior Blair, Frank McCain, David Richmond, and Joseph McNeil—could take pride in their leadership. But they knew they hadn't won the final victory. Segregation was still the rule in Greensboro and throughout the South, where many restaurants, movie theaters, and hotels kept their doors closed to black Americans. The struggle for equality wasn't finished.

> **"The Greensboro sit-in was successful in righting a wrong."**
>
> —*Ralph Johns, Greensboro businessman, 1979*

CHAPTER 8

PRESIDENTS AND POLITICS

It ought to be possible for American consumers of any color to receive equal service in . . . hotels and restaurants and theaters and retail stores, without being forced to resort to demonstrations in the street."

—President John F. Kennedy, address on civil rights, June 11, 1963

On July 26, 1960, under the bold headline "Sit-Ins Victorious," the *New York Times* announced that store managers in Greensboro had desegregated their lunch counters. Over the following months, journalists wrote occasional reports on the continuing progress of the sit-in movement, but the national news spotlight shifted to the presidential election. John F. Kennedy and Richard M. Nixon were the candidates representing the two dominant political parties. Which man stood for civil rights? voters wondered. Which one would best support the struggle for equality?

John F. Kennedy, Democrat *(left)*, and Richard M. Nixon, Republican *(right)*, were facing each other in the election for president of the United States in 1960.

KENNEDY VERSUS NIXON

Kennedy and Nixon had much in common. Both were experienced politicians. Nixon, the Republican Party candidate, had served in the U.S. House of Representatives and the Senate. He then served as vice president for eight years under President Dwight D. Eisenhower. Kennedy, the Democratic Party candidate, had also been a representative and a senator. Both Nixon and Kennedy made foreign policy the main campaign issue. Each discussed how he would fight the Cold War, the contest between Communist nations led by the USSR and non-Communist nations led by the United States.

Nixon and Kennedy had good reasons for directing attention to foreign policy. U.S. citizens might not have agreed on how to fight the Cold War, but they generally believed the United States had to defeat Communism. Domestic issues, such as crime, housing, education, and health care, were more controversial. No matter what a candidate said about these issues, he was certain to make enemies because voters disagreed about what the problems were and how to find solutions.

Civil rights was one such controversial issue, especially in southern states. Nixon and Kennedy assumed that white southerners opposed desegregation while black southerners supported it. White voters outnumbered black voters. Consequently, both candidates tried to avoid upsetting white voters. Nixon, for example, made a point of saying that he had never joined or donated money to the NAACP. Kennedy, meanwhile, chose a white southerner, Senator Lyndon B. Johnson of Texas, as the Democratic candidate for vice president.

Despite the similarities between Nixon and Kennedy, voters could pick up clues about each man's commitment to civil rights. Recent history showed that Republican presidents hadn't done much for African Americans. Voters remembered President Eisenhower's reluctance to enforce the U.S. Supreme Court's call for school desegregation. He thought desegregation was a problem the citizens of each town had to work out on their own, without interference from the federal government.

Nixon clearly shared this view, yet he attempted to assure voters that he did care about civil rights. During the campaign, he paid a visit to a new landmark in the struggle for equality: Greensboro, North Carolina.

Presidential candidate Richard Nixon checks out the crowd in Greensboro during a campaign stop in August 1960.

More than ten thousand people came to hear his speech. Eisenhower and other Republicans had the best civil rights policy, Nixon declared. They understood that legislation couldn't end segregation because a law was useless if citizens didn't support it. Instead of demanding action from Congress or the president, community leaders should take action themselves. In this way, Nixon claimed, Americans would solve the problem of segregation through voluntary efforts.

But what, exactly, did Nixon's call for voluntary action mean? Was he saying that, if elected, he would urge local leaders to work for civil rights? Or was he suggesting that civil rights weren't the president's responsibility? There was no doubt that Nixon didn't think the federal government should become involved.

Taking the opposite view, the Democratic Party believed the federal government should actively protect and care for U.S. citizens. Democratic presidents had a better record on civil rights than the

Republicans. Franklin D. Roosevelt had included African Americans in job programs in the 1930s. During World War II, he forbade corporations with government contracts to discriminate against black employees. After the war, President Harry S. Truman ended segregation in the military. African Americans wondered whether Kennedy would follow the example of these presidents if voters elected him in 1960.

Kennedy suggested that he would indeed involve the federal government in the struggle for equality. During a debate with Nixon in September, he pointed out that African Americans did not have equal rights, opportunities, and freedoms. Compared to white citizens, black citizens had fewer opportunities to attend college, own a house, or get a dependable job. But Kennedy, like Nixon, sent an ambiguous message.

On the one hand, Kennedy assured voters that he understood the problems facing African Americans. On the other hand, he didn't spell out a solution for those problems. He was careful not to alienate voters who wanted to preserve the status quo.

Throughout the summer and early fall of 1960, both Kennedy and Nixon sidled away from controversial issues. Then, in mid-October, with the election only a few weeks away, an event forced the candidates to decide whether or not they would take a strong stand on civil rights. Martin Luther King Jr. was arrested in Atlanta during a sit-in. Although the protesters had not used violence, the judge handed King an extremely harsh sentence. Voters wondered how Kennedy and Nixon would respond.

▓ ▓ ▓ ▓ A PHONE CALL

King's arrest was part of a plan designed by student protesters to make the struggle for equality national news. Under pressure from the sit-in movement, store managers in Nashville, Greensboro, and many other southern cities had opened their lunch counters to black customers. Yet store managers in Atlanta refused to desegregate, so students kept protesting. Hoping to draw attention, they urged King to join them for a sit-in at Rich's department store. King was a national figure. His speeches and activities made headlines. If he participated in the sit-in, students knew, reporters would come.

During the 1960 presidential election campaign, Democrat John F. Kennedy ran against Republican Richard M. Nixon. The Cold War between the United States, the leading democratic nation, and the Union of Soviet Socialist Republics (USSR), the leading Communist nation, was an important issue throughout the campaign. During a debate with Nixon on September 26, Kennedy referred to Communism as "slavery" and democracy as "freedom." At the same time, he pointed out that the United States did not treat all citizens equally. African Americans did not have the same rights, opportunities, and freedoms that other Americans did. "I'm not satisfied until every American enjoys his full constitutional rights," Kennedy said. "I think we can do better. I don't want the talents of any American to go to waste."

In his response to Kennedy, Nixon did not specifically mention African Americans. However, he assured the television audience: "We [the Republican Party] are for programs that will expand educational opportunities, that will give to all Americans their equal chance for education, for all of the things which are necessary and dear to the hearts of our people."

Protesters may have had a second reason for inviting King. Hundreds of students had been arrested since the beginning of the sit-in movement. Many had chosen to pay bail, but many others had followed King's advice and chosen to serve time in jail. Perhaps the Atlanta students were challenging King to follow his own advice.

Martin Luther King Jr. *(center)* **and his wife, Coretta Scott King** *(kissing his cheek),* **celebrate with family and supporters after his release from jail in October 1960.**

King accepted the invitation to join a sit-in on October 19. As predicted, when Atlanta police arrested the protesters, he boldly vowed to serve whatever sentence the judge gave him—even if it was ten years. A few days later, store owners dropped the charges. The protesters were immediately released from jail. Instead of freeing King, however, the judge sentenced him to four months of hard labor on a road gang. King had been arrested in May 1960 for a minor traffic offense and put on probation. According to the judge, King had violated probation by participating in the sit-in. Therefore, the jail sentence was justified.

Assuming the majority of white southerners were happy about the sentence, both Nixon and Kennedy took care not to alienate these voters. Nixon made no comment on King's arrest or imprisonment. Kennedy said nothing in public either, but he did take action. On October 26, he made a phone call to Coretta Scott King, who was obviously worried about her husband. She was also expecting a baby, and she already had two small children to care for. After John Kennedy called Mrs. King to offer encouragement, his brother and assistant, Robert Kennedy, called the judge who had handed down the harsh sentence. The judge reconsidered his decision and released the famous prisoner the next day.

The Democratic Party quickly sent a pamphlet to black voters, telling them what the Kennedys had done for King and his wife. King thanked John Kennedy publicly but refused to campaign for him. However, King's father, the well-known minister Martin Luther King Sr., announced that he would vote for Kennedy and urged other blacks to do the same.

The students' plan had worked. By convincing King to participate in a sit-in, they had drawn national attention to the protests in Atlanta and given the candidates an opportunity to address the issue of civil rights. Kennedy's phone call to Mrs. King apparently helped his campaign because, in November 1960, voters elected him the next president.

Martin Luther King Sr., also a well-known minister, announced his support for John F. Kennedy in 1960.

PRESIDENT KENNEDY

When Kennedy took office in early 1961, many Americans expected him to support the struggle for equality with new federal laws and strong federal action. They soon found that the president had a different list of priorities. Fighting the Cold War against the USSR was at the top of that list. He had to decide how the United States would respond to military crises around the world. At the same time, he negotiated with the Soviet leader, Nikita Khrushchev, in an effort to bring peace.

Another item high on Kennedy's list of priorities was government assistance for needy citizens. He predicted a long battle with Congress because his plans for welfare, health care, and housing would demand tax dollars. As an experienced politician, Kennedy carefully weighed the odds. He decided not to risk losing support for his social welfare programs by asking Congress to pass civil rights legislation. He may have reasoned that African Americans, who had high rates of poverty and unemployment, would benefit from the new government programs.

Despite his reluctance to push for civil rights legislation, Kennedy worked to end racial discrimination within the federal government. He appointed well-known African Americans to important posts. When he needed a judge for a federal court in New York, he nominated Thurgood Marshall, the lawyer who had won the 1954 court case *Brown v. Board of Education.* Kennedy also created the Committee on Equal Employment Opportunity, which pressured federal agencies and corporations with federal contracts to hire black employees.

Kennedy and his wife, Jacqueline, demonstrated that they held no prejudices against African Americans. Setting an example for the rest of the nation, the president and the first lady frequently entertained black guests at the White House. President Kennedy also refused to belong to clubs that didn't allow black members.

In contrast to the president, Robert Kennedy gave civil rights top priority. When his brother appointed him U.S. attorney general, he hired new staff members for the Civil Rights Division of the Justice Department. They investigated reports of discrimination, pressed lawsuits against offenders, and demanded enforcement of court orders. Across the United States, the Justice Department team worked to safeguard voting rights and to end school segregation.

For Americans seeking equality, however, the Kennedys weren't moving fast enough. The president, worried about politics in Congress, gave civil rights legislation low priority. Although the attorney general tried to speed lawsuits through

Robert F. Kennedy, U.S. attorney general, speaks to a crowd of equal rights supporters in Washington, D.C., in 1963.

the courts, he had to follow time-consuming legal procedures. Once again, political and legal tactics had proven ineffective; and civil rights activists turned to the tactics of nonviolent protest.

■ A TIME OF PROTEST

New protests began with Freedom Rides. In 1946 the U.S. Supreme Court had forbidden segregation on buses running on interstate routes. In 1960, in the case *Boynton v. Virginia*, the Court had ruled that segregation in bus stations, restrooms, and other facilities for travelers was also illegal. To see if southern officials would respect the Court's decision, a group of black passengers and white passengers in Washington, D.C., boarded a bus bound for New Orleans in the spring of 1961. They were determined to challenge Jim Crow customs and cross the lines of segregation both on the bus and at every terminal along the way.

A group of CORE Freedom Riders map out their route in Washington, D.C., in May 1961. They planned to challenge segregation in southern bus stations.

As the Freedom Riders traveled through the South, they were threatened and beaten by opponents of desegregation. When the original passengers couldn't go on, new volunteers stepped in, and the Freedom Rides continued throughout the summer. So did the violence. At last, Robert Kennedy and his Justice Department team moved to enforce the U.S. Supreme Court decision outlawing segregation.

Freedom riders sit on their luggage at a bus station in Birmingham, Alabama, in May 1961, waiting to continue their journey for desegregation.

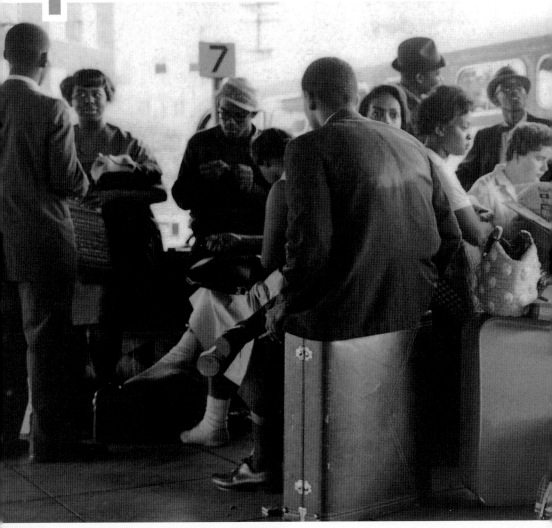

Just as the Freedom Rides came to an end in the fall of 1961, civil rights leaders in Albany, Georgia, organized sit-ins and marches to protest segregation. When this protest movement fizzled out in failure in late 1962, they blamed President Kennedy's refusal to get involved. Perhaps he didn't see a need for federal intervention because the demonstrations were relatively peaceful. In contrast to police officers in many southern cities, the Albany police did not attack the protesters.

Washington, D.C., May 4, 1961: Thirteen volunteers—seven blacks and six whites—depart on two buses for New Orleans. They plan to see if southern authorities will respect the federal laws and court decisions banning segregation on interstate transportation.

Rock Hill, South Carolina, May 9: Two riders are beaten.

Anniston, Alabama, May 14: Outside of town, segregationists set fire to the first bus and beat the passengers. Passengers on the second bus are beaten at the bus terminal, but they continue on to Birmingham, Alabama.

Birmingham, May 14 [same day]: Riders on the second bus are beaten. This time, they're unable to go on.

Birmingham, May 17: When a new group of volunteers from Nashville arrives, they are arrested by Birmingham police. As soon as they are released, they return to continue the Freedom Ride with another set of reinforcements.

The Freedom Rides—and the violence—continue across the South throughout the summer of 1961.

James Meredith *(center, holding briefcase)* is surrounded by federal marshals as he arrives to register at the University of Mississippi in September 1962.

Only violence, it seemed, could force the president to speak out. When a bloody riot erupted in Oxford, Mississippi, in September 1962, Kennedy responded by sending troops. James Meredith had attempted to enroll at the University of Mississippi, which had never admitted a black student. The state governor swore to defend this Mississippi tradition and gave a speech on the radio to stir up segregationists. Expecting trouble, Robert Kennedy sent five hundred federal marshals to campus to protect Meredith. Throughout the night of September 30, the marshals fought off a mob. Although the mob threw bricks and fired shotguns, the marshals defended themselves using only tear gas and clubs. At least one hundred fifty marshals were injured. Twenty-five were killed. That was enough for Kennedy. In the morning, he called out the army. With five thousand soldiers on campus, the riot quickly ended; and Meredith started classes.

A teenaged civil rights demonstrator is attacked by a police dog in Birmingham on May 3, 1963. Photos of this kind of violence led President Kennedy to send troops to quiet Birmingham.

Eight months later, President Kennedy again called out the army to end violence. In April 1963, Martin Luther King Jr. led a protest movement against segregation in Birmingham, Alabama. The Birmingham police attacked protesters with clubs, dogs, and water hoses. Thousands of protesters—including hundreds of schoolchildren—were arrested, and

King spent Easter weekend in jail. Despite King's pleas for nonviolence, under the unrelenting attacks of their opponents, some protesters turned to violence. On May 12, 1963, when it looked as though Birmingham would explode in a racial war, Kennedy sent troops to surround the city. The rioting stopped immediately, and Birmingham's leaders agreed to open public schools, libraries, parks, and lunch counters to all citizens.

The violence in Birmingham and Oxford at last convinced Kennedy that he couldn't delay any longer. On June 11, 1963, the president went on television to talk to Americans. The struggle for equality had turned into a protest movement, he explained, because current laws were unjust. Clearly the nation needed a new law guaranteeing the rights of every person. He promised to ask Congress for such a law, and he asked citizens to follow it. Together, they would make the United States a truly free, democratic country. A week later, just as Kennedy had promised, he urged Congress to create legislation safeguarding voting rights and outlawing segregation in all public places.

While Congress debated the provisions of the new law, civil rights leaders planned a huge, nonviolent protest in Washington. By holding a mass march in the nation's capital, these leaders intended to show the strength of their supporters and keep gentle pressure on Kennedy. The SCLC, CORE, and other key civil rights organizations collaborated in planning the march. The national leaders of the NAACP, who had hesitated to support the student sit-ins only three years earlier, agreed to participate in the protest march.

Leaders of SNCC participated as well. Since its founding in April 1960, SNCC had proven that young people could contribute to the struggle for equality. Sit-in leaders volunteered as bus passengers during the Freedom Rides, and college students had joined the protests in Albany and Birmingham. Most important, SNCC workers in the South ran a campaign to register black voters. As a result, SNCC had emerged as a strong force for civil rights.

On August 28, 1963, more than two hundred fifty thousand protesters joined the March on Washington. They met at the Lincoln Memorial, a landmark symbol of freedom. John Lewis, the chairman of SNCC, was one of many civil rights leaders who addressed the crowd.

Martin Luther King Jr. *(front row, second from left)* walks with more than 250,000 civil rights activists during the 1963 March on Washington.

That day Dr. King gave the most famous speech of his life, "I have a dream."

The March on Washington was a great success, and President Kennedy praised the protesters for their nonviolent demonstration. Although he had decided not to give a speech at the Lincoln Memorial, he hosted a reception at the White House for the organizers of the march. In late August 1963, civil rights leaders could feel confident that the president stood for their cause.

Just three months later, on November 22, 1963, John F. Kennedy was assassinated. With Kennedy's death, Vice President Lyndon B. Johnson suddenly became President Johnson. Grieving Americans wondered where this politician from Texas put civil rights on his list of priorities.

Martin Luther King Jr. gives his famous "I have a dream" speech at the Lincoln Memorial in Washington, D.C., on August 28, 1963.

■ ■ ■ ■ A VICTORY FOR CIVIL RIGHTS

Johnson immediately took up Kennedy's campaign for new civil rights legislation. As a former senator, Johnson knew how Congress operated. He knew that, although members of Congress wouldn't risk bad publicity by voting against the civil rights bill, they could defeat it in other ways. They could set up committees and hold endless debates without ever taking a vote. Alternatively, they could work out a compromise by rewriting and weakening the bill so that it would be more acceptable to opponents. A member of Congress could then tell black voters that he or she had supported the new law while assuring segregationists that it didn't threaten the status quo.

Johnson, however, refused to allow the bill to die in committee or to suffer a debilitating compromise. Working with key civil rights leaders and using his own contacts in the Senate, Johnson put pressure on Congress to approve a strong civil rights bill as quickly as possible. Despite a grueling debate, the bill passed both the House of Representatives and the Senate. On July 2, Johnson signed the Civil Rights Act of 1964 into law. In addition to implementing school integration, the act prohibited segregation in all public places.

The Civil Rights Act of 1964 was a legacy of John F. Kennedy, the candidate who had dared to show support for Martin Luther King Jr. during the 1960 presidential campaign. The new law was also a legacy of the sit-in movement. Using the tactics of nonviolent protest, young men and women had called attention to discrimination against black Americans.

President Lyndon B. Johnson *(front right)* signs the historic Civil Rights Act of 1964. The law forbids segregation in public places.

The Civil Rights Act of 1964 was a victory for every American who participated in the sit-in movement. In addition to provisions for voting rights and school integration, the law included a section outlawing segregation in public places.

RELIEF AGAINST DISCRIMINATION IN PLACES OF PUBLIC ACCOMMODATION

SEC. 201.

(a)

All persons shall be entitled to the full and equal enjoyment of the goods, services, facilities, and privileges, advantages, and accommodations of any place of public accommodation, as defined in this section, without discrimination or segregation on the ground of race, color, religion, or national origin.

(b) . . .

(1) any inn, hotel, motel, or other establishment which provides lodging to transient guests, . . . (2) any restaurant, cafeteria, lunchroom, lunch counter, soda fountain, or other facility principally engaged in selling food for consumption on the premises . . .

(3) any motion picture house, theater, concert hall, sports arena, stadium or other place of exhibition or entertainment . . .

Their courageous persistence had made segregation a national issue and eventually scored a victory in the struggle for equality. Less than five years after the Greensboro Four sat down at a lunch counter, restaurants, stores, hotels, stadiums, theaters, and other businesses across the United States were required by law to give all customers equal service.

LEARNING TO LIVE TOGETHER

I enjoy going back there now and seeing the black people drink coffee just the same as anybody else."

—General James Richard Townsend, Greensboro city manager, 1978

The four freshmen from A&T College who started a sit-in at the Woolworth's lunch counter in Greensboro, North Carolina, in February 1960, showed not only that nonviolent protest was effective but also that anyone could join the struggle for equality. Those young men launched a movement that spread throughout the United States and attracted thousands of supporters. By the end of 1960, store managers in Greensboro, Nashville, and several other southern cities had opened their lunch counters to black customers. The protest against segregation continued with Freedom Rides, boycotts, picket lines, and the famous March on Washington. In response, Congress passed the federal Civil Rights Act of 1964, outlawing segregation in all public places.

(Left to right) Joseph McNeil, Jibreel Khazan (formerly Ezell Blair Jr.), Franklin McCain, and David Richmond again sit at the Woolworth's lunch counter in Greensboro in August 1990 to commemorate the thirtieth anniversary of their sit-in.

Since the 1960s, African Americans, Latino Americans, Native Americans, Asian Americans, women, and other minority groups have employed a combination of tactics in the struggle for equality. Political and legal tactics remain important. On occasion, nonviolent protest is effective because it draws attention to discrimination and injustice. Increasingly, minorities turn to voting, lobbying, and political activism in order to achieve their goals. At the same time, men and women from minority groups are holding more offices at every level of government. Clarence Thomas, an African American, is a U.S. Supreme Court justice.

INTERNATIONAL CIVIL RIGHTS CENTER AND MUSEUM

In 1960 the Woolworth's store in Greensboro, North Carolina, was a place where blacks faced discrimination. In 2010 that same building on South Elm Street is the International Civil Rights Center and Museum. It is a place where Americans can remember the racial injustices of the past and celebrate the courage of the men and women who joined the struggle for freedom and equality.

The vision for this museum began with two men: Melvin "Skip" Alston, a county commissioner, and Earl Jones, a member of the state legislature. When the Woolworth's store closed in 1993, Alston and Jones created Sit-in Movement Inc. in order to raise funds to convert the building into a museum. It took seventeen years and $23 million to make their vision a reality. On February 1, 2010—the fiftieth anniversary of the famous Greensboro sit-in—the museum officially opened.

The museum's centerpiece is the original lunch counter where Junior Blair and his friends protested segregation. If you visit the museum, you can share their experience by watching a film dramatization of their dorm-room discussions and walking through a hall representing the

Condoleeza Rice, an African American woman, served as U.S. secretary of state. Bill Richardson, a Latino, has been the governor of New Mexico. In addition, many members of Congress belong to minority groups.

In the twenty-first century, although inequalities persist in education, housing, and employment, there are signs that Americans are learning to live together. Perhaps the most promising of these signs is the election of Barack Obama. In January 2009, Obama became the first African American to hold the office of president of the United States. Many Americans believe that, with his leadership, they can work together to win equality for all.

streets of Greensboro. Along the way, you pass pictures of civil rights heroes who inspired the four young men. When you reach the lunch counter, videos let you imagine that you are part of the sit-in. Although the museum focuses on the history of civil rights in the United States, exhibits remind visitors that the struggle for justice and equality continues all over the world.

A section of lunch counter from the Greensboro Woolworth's can also be found at the National Museum of American History, Smithsonian Institution, in Washington, D.C.

The original Woolworth's lunch counter is on view at the International Civil Rights Center and Museum in Greensboro *(below)*. Another section is at the Smithsonian in Washington, D.C.

1849: Henry David Thoreau publishes the essay "Civil Disobedience."

1861: Abraham Lincoln becomes president of the United States. The U.S. Civil War begins.

1863: President Lincoln issues the Emancipation Proclamation abolishing slavery in states that seceded from the Union.

1865: The U.S. Civil War ends. The Thirteenth Amendment to the U.S. Constitution abolishes slavery throughout the nation.

1868: The Fourteenth Amendment to the U.S. Constitution forbids state governments from denying the rights of any citizen.

1870: The Fifteenth Amendment to the U.S. Constitution guarantees the right to vote for all male citizens aged 21 and older.

1896: In the case *Plessy v. Ferguson*, the U.S. Supreme Court establishes the doctrine of "separate but equal."

1909: The National Association for the Advancement of Colored People (NAACP) is founded.

1941: President Roosevelt issues Executive Order 8802 banning racial discrimination in the defense industry. The United States enters World War II.

1945: Roosevelt dies. Harry S. Truman becomes president. World War II ends.

1948: President Truman issues Executive Order 9981 mandating desegregation of the military. The United Nations issues the Universal Declaration of Human Rights.

1954: In the case *Brown v. Board of Education*, the U.S. Supreme Court bans segregation in public schools.

1955–1956: Black Americans boycott segregated city buses in Montgomery, Alabama.

1957: A riot breaks out when black students attempt to desegregate Central High School in Little Rock, Arkansas. The Civil Rights Act of 1957 creates the Civil Rights Commission to study the issues and protect voting rights.

1960: In February the sit-in movement begins in Greensboro, North Carolina. In April leaders of the sit-in movement founded the Student Nonviolent Coordinating Committee (SNCC). In July store managers in Greensboro desegregate the lunch counters.

1961: President John F. Kennedy becomes president. The Freedom Rides test laws forbidding segregation on public interstate transportation.

1963: In June President Kennedy calls for civil rights legislation. In August the March on Washington demonstrates widespread support for the civil rights movement. In November Kennedy is assassinated, and Lyndon B. Johnson becomes president.

1964: The Civil Rights Act of 1964 prohibits segregation in all public places.

2010: The International Civil Rights Center and Museum opens in Greensboro.

Ella Baker

(1903–1986) Baker was a civil rights activist from North Carolina. She served as the executive director of the Southern Christian Leadership Conference (SCLC) from 1958 to 1960. She wanted to help the young men and women who participated in the sit-ins, but she didn't want other civil rights groups to take over the student movement. For this reason, she invited student leaders to a conference in April 1960. With her encouragement, they started an organization of their own.

Ezell Blair Jr.

(1941–) Blair was a student at A&T College in Greensboro, North Carolina, who launched the sit-in movement in 1960. He was born and raised in Greensboro. He took a leadership role throughout the sit-in movement and attended the founding meeting of the Student Nonviolent Coordinating Committee. After graduating from A&T, Blair worked for the AFL-CIO and other labor organizations. He also served as a counselor for persons with disabilities. When he converted to Islam in the late 1960s, he changed his name to Jebreel Khazan. He continues to work for civil rights.

Caesar Cone

(1908–) Cone was a Greensboro businessman who exemplified paternalism toward African Americans. He donated $50,000 for the construction of a YMCA. Yet this YMCA was exclusively for blacks because they weren't allowed to use the YMCA for whites. Cone also hired black workers, but they were allowed at only one of his textile mills because he didn't think blacks and whites should work side by side.

Luther Hodges

(1898–1974) Hodges was governor of North Carolina from 1954 to 1960. He turned school desegregation into a political issue in order to win reelection. Hodges opposed the *Brown v. Board of Education* decision. He said the residents of each school district—not the U.S. Supreme Court—had the right to decide if black students and white students should attend classes together. His plan, which he called "voluntary segregation," delayed school desegregation throughout the state.

Thurgood Marshall

(1908–1993) Marshall was a lawyer and judge from Maryland. As a lawyer for the NAACP, he represented African American students and their families in *Brown v. Board of Education* (1954), the case in which the U.S. Supreme Court outlawed segregation in public schools. He became the first African American to serve as a justice on the U.S. Supreme Court. Although Marshall supported the student protesters during the sit-in movement, he thought that they should pay bail instead of serving time in jail when they were arrested.

Franklin McCain

(1942–) McCain was a student at A&T College in Greensboro, North Carolina, who launched the sit-in movement in 1960. McCain was born in North Carolina, but he grew up in Washington, D.C. During the sit-in movement, he participated in the negotiations between Greensboro's business leaders and the students. Soon after graduating from A&T, McCain moved to Charlotte, North Carolina, where he took a job as a chemist. Still dedicated to the struggle for equality, he participates in many local civic organizations, including the regional branch of the NAACP.

Joseph McNeil

(1942–) McNeil was a student at A&T College in Greensboro, North Carolina, who launched the sit-in movement in 1960. He grew up in North Carolina. McNeil received a full scholarship to A&T, where he studied physics and participated in the ROTC program. In 1963, after graduation, he joined the U.S. Air Force. Although he also worked for the Federal Aviation Administration for most of his career, he remained in the U.S. Air Force Reserve and earned the rank of major general.

National Association for the Advancement of Colored People (NAACP)

The NAACP was founded in 1909 by W. E. B. Dubois to promote the rights of African Americans. At first, leaders of the NAACP hesitated to show support for the sit-in movement because they feared the protests would trigger a backlash of racism against blacks. Eventually, though, the NAACP leaders agreed that nonviolent protest could be effective.

Willa Player

(1909–2003) A native of Mississippi, Player was president of Bennett College for Women in Greensboro, North Carolina, from 1956 to 1966. During the sit-ins, some of Greensboro's community leaders thought that Player should try to stop the protests by disciplining students who participated in them. Player refused. Instead of punishing the protesters, she encouraged all citizens to work together.

David Richmond

(c.1942–1990) Richmond was a student at A&T College in Greensboro, North Carolina, who launched the sit-in movement in 1960. He grew up in Greensboro. While he was in college, he planned to become a minister. Richmond spent most of his adult life in Greensboro, although he constantly faced discrimination. Because of his brave leadership role in the sit-in movement, some people unjustly considered him a troublemaker. Nonetheless, in 1980, the Greensboro Chamber of Commerce gave him an award for promoting human rights.

Claude Sitton

(1925–) Sitton was a staff journalist for the *New York Times*. He covered events in the southern states, and he made the sit-ins national news. In his articles, he tried to include the perspective of the protesters as well as the perspective of their opponents. During the early years of the civil rights movement, news reports by Sitton and other journalists encouraged many Americans to join the struggle for equality.

Student Nonviolent Coordinating Committee (SNCC)

In April 1960, student leaders of the sit-in movement created SNCC (pronounced "Snick") in order to share ideas and information. Although the founders emphasized nonviolence, in the mid-1960s, some leaders of SNCC called for more aggressive forms of protest.

Edward Zane

(1899–1991) Zane was a business executive and member of the Greensboro City Council. He took the student protesters seriously, and he won their trust. By negotiating with store managers, city officials, and leaders of the African American community, Zane helped to end segregation at many public places in Greensboro.

accredit: to officially recognize that an institution or a person meets a set of standards

amendment: a change or alteration made to a written constitution

assassinate: to murder for political reasons

boycott: a means of protest in which consumers refuse to buy a company's products because of its policies

***Brown v. Board of Education* (1954):** the U.S. Supreme Court case that declared school segregation unconstitutional

Civil Rights Act of 1964: federal law prohibiting racial segregation and mandating fair voting regulations

Cold War: the political and cultural conflict between the United States and the USSR during the twentieth century (1945–1991)

Communism: a system of government based on the belief that the wealth and resources of a nation belong equally to all of its citizens

democracy: a form of government normally executed through majority rule and a system of elected representatives

desegregation: the process or act of ending segregation

discrimination: unequal treatment based on physical or social differences and not on merit

jail-in: a form of nonviolent protest. Protesters who are arrested choose to serve time in jail in order to demonstrate their commitment to a cause.

Ku Klux Klan (KKK): a group that supports white supremacy

manumission: the formal act of releasing a person from slavery

moratorium: a planned suspension of a conflict in order to allow time for negotiation

National Association for the Advancement of Colored People (NAACP): one of the United States' oldest civil rights organizations, the NAACP was formed in 1909 to work against racial discrimination

***Plessy v. Ferguson* (1896):** the U.S. Supreme Court case that upheld segregation under the rule "separate but equal"

prejudice: a preconceived judgment or adverse opinion against a person or a group

propaganda: information intended to influence attitudes toward an institution, a cause, or a person

Reconstruction: the era after the Civil War from 1865 to 1877 when the governments and societies of the former Confederate states were occupied by U.S. troops, rebuilt, and allowed to rejoin the Union by fulfilling certain requirements

segregation: the forced separation of different groups, based on race, religion, or other criteria. In the South, the separation of black citizens from white citizens was known as Jim Crow and was practiced until the 1960s.

sit-in: an organized, nonviolent form of protest. Protesters occupy a space forbidden to them.

Supreme Court of the United States: the highest judicial body within the U.S. judicial system

token desegregation: the inclusion of a small number of persons representing a minority group in an organization where most persons represent the dominant group in society. For example, in the South, local school boards permitted a few black students to attend schools exclusively for white students in order to satisfy the U.S. Supreme Court's demand for school desegregation.

6   Willa B. Player, interviewed by
     Eugene Pfaff, Greensboro Voices,
     Jackson Library, University of
     North Carolina at Greensboro,
     December 3, 1979. Available
     online at http://library.uncg.edu/
     depts/archives/civrights/detail-
     iv.asp?iv=115 (May 24, 2010).

17   Ezell Blair Jr., (Jibreel Khazan)
     and Franklin McCain,
     interviewed by Eugene Pfaff,
     Greensboro Voices, October 20,
     1979. Available online at http://
     library.uncg.edu/depts/archives/
     civrights/detail-iv.asp?iv=76
     (May 24, 2010).

18   Jo Jones Spivey, interviewed by
     Eugene Pfaff, Greensboro Voices,
     May 30, 1979. Available online at
     http://library.uncg.edu/depts/
     archives/civrights/detail-iv
     .asp?iv=132 (May 24, 2010).

20   "Constitution of the United
     States," Amendments 11–27,
     National Archives and Records
     Administration, n.d., http://
     www.archives.gov/exhibits/
     charters/constitution_
     amendments_11-27.html (May
     21, 2010).

22   "Emancipation Proclamation,"
     National Archives and Records
     Administration, n.d., http://
     www.archives.gov/exhibits/
     featured_documents/
     emancipation_proclamation/
     transcript.html (May 1, 2010).

29   "Executive Order 9981:
     Desegregation of the Armed
     Forces (1948)," Our Documents,
     n.d., http://www.our
     documents.gov/doc
     .php?flash=false&doc=84 (May
     1, 2010).

30–31 "United Nations Declaration of

Human Rights," United Nations,
n.d., http://www.un.org/en/
documents/udhr/ (May 1, 2010).

36   Otis Hairston Sr., interviewed by
     Eugene Pfaff, Greensboro Voices,
     June 1, 1979. Available online at
     http://library.uncg.edu/depts/
     archives/civrights/detail-iv
     .asp?iv=51 (May 24, 2010).

38   "Plessy v. Ferguson (1896)," Our
     Documents, n.d., http://www
     .ourdocuments.gov/doc
     .php?flash=false&doc=52 (May
     1, 2010).

50   Spivey interview, Greensboro
     Voices.

53   Henry David Thoreau, Civil
     Disobedience, The Thoreau Reader,
     n.d., http://thoreau.eserver.org/
     civil.html (May 12, 2010).

61   Ralph Johns, interviewed by
     Eugene Pfaff, Greensboro Voices,
     January 17, 1979. Available online
     at http://library.uncg.edu/depts/
     archives/civrights/detail-iv
     .asp?iv=72 (May 24, 2010).

64   Robert Tyrone Patterson,
     interviewed by William Link,
     Greensboro Voices, April 24,
     1989. Available online at http://
     library.uncg.edu/depts/archives/
     civrights/detail-iv.asp?iv=113
     (May 24, 2010).

66   Blair and McCain interview,
     Greensboro Voices.

69   Patterson interview, Greensboro
     Voices.

74   Ibid.

77   Edward R. Zane, interviewed
     by William Link, Greensboro
     Voices, February 13, 1987.
     Available online at http://
     library.uncg.edu/depts/archives/
     civrights/detail-iv.asp?iv=148
     (May 24, 2010).

79 Joseph McNeil, interviewed by Eugene Pfaff, Greensboro Voices, October 14, 1979. Available online at http://library.uncg.edu/depts/archives/civrights/detail-iv.asp?iv=100 (May 24, 2010).

80 Blair and McCain interview, Greensboro Voices.

82 McNeil interview, Greensboro Voices.

87 Blair and McCain interview, Greensboro Voices.

89 Johns interview, Greensboro Voices.

92 Otis L. Hairston Sr. and Nelson Napoleon Johnson, interviewed by William Link, Greensboro Voices, May 5, 1989. Available online at http://library.uncg.edu/depts/archives/civrights/detail-iv.asp?iv=53 (May 24, 2010).

99 Blair and McCain interview, Greensboro Voices.

100 Ibid.

115 Johns interview, Greensboro Voices.

116 "Radio and Television Report to the American People on Civil Rights," June 11, 1963, JFKlink.com, 2004, http://www.jfklink.com/speeches/jfk/publicpapers/1963/jfk237_63.html (May 6, 2010).

121 "Senator John F. Kennedy and Vice President Richard M. Nixon: First Joint Radio-Television Broadcast," September 26, 1960, JFKlink.com, 2004, http://www.jfklink.com/speeches/joint/joint260960_1st_Debate.html (May 6, 2010).

121 Ibid.

135 "Civil Rights Act (1964)," Our Documents, n.d., http://www.ourdocuments.gov/doc.php?flash=false&doc=97 (May 22, 2010).

138 James Richard Townsend, interviewed by Eugene Pfaff, Greensboro Voices, November 22, 1978. Available online at http://library.uncg.edu/depts/archives/civrights/detail-iv.asp?iv=142 (May 24, 2010).

Amar, Akhil Reed. *America's Constitution, A Biography*. New York: Random House, 2005.

Arnett, Ethel Stephens. *Greensboro North Carolina: The County Seat of Guilford*. Written under the direction of Walter Clinton Jackson. Chapel Hill: University of North Carolina Press, 1955.

Berg, Manfred. "Black Civil Rights and Liberal Anticommunism: The NAACP in the Early Cold War." *Journal of American History* 94, no. 1 (June 2007): 75–96.

Branch, Taylor. *Parting the Waters: America in the King Years, 1954–1963*. New York: Simon and Schuster, 1988.

Bureau of Census, United States Department of Commerce, *18th Decennial Census of the United States, Census of Population 1960*. Vol. 1, *Characteristics of the Population, Part 35, North Carolina*. Washington, DC: Government Printing Office, 1963.

Carson, Clayborne. *In Struggle: SNCC and the Black Awakening of the 1960s*. Cambridge, MA: Harvard University Press, 1995.

Chafe, William H. *Civilities and Civil Rights: Greensboro, North Carolina and the Black Struggle for Freedom*. New York: Oxford University Press, 1980.

————. *The Unfinished Journey: America Since World War II*. 6th ed. New York: Oxford University Press, 2007.

Coski, John M. *The Confederate Battle Flag: America's Most Embattled Emblem*. Cambridge, MA: The Belknap Press of Harvard University Press, 2005.

Davis, Art. *City Trends: U.S. Census, 1960-1990: Greensboro, N.C.* Greensboro: Department of Planning and Community Development, 1993.

Gandhi, film directed by Richard Attenborough, 1982.

Garraty, John A., and Mark C. Carnes. *The American Nation: A History of the United States*. 10th ed. New York: Longman, 2000.

Gross, Robert. "Quiet War with the State: Henry David Thoreau and Civil Disobedience." *Yale Review* 91 (October 2005): 1–17.

Hampton, Henry, and Steve Fayer, eds. (with Sarah Flynn). *Voices of Freedom: An Oral History of the Civil Rights Movement from the 1950s through the 1980s*. New York: Bantam Books, 1990.

Hogan, Wesley. *Many Minds, One Heart: SNCC's Dream for a New America*. Chapel Hill: University of North Carolina Press, 2007.

Lewis, George. *Massive Resistance: The White Response to the Civil Rights Movement*. New York: Oxford University Press, 2006.

Meier, August, Elliott Rudwick, and Francis L. Broderick, eds. *Black Protest Thought in the Twentieth Century*. 2nd ed. New York: The Bobbs-Merrill Company, Inc., 1971.

Patterson, James T. *Grand Expectations: The United States, 1945–1974.* New York: Oxford University Press, 1996.

Pitrone, Jean Maddern. *F.W. Woolworth and the American Five and Dime: A Social History.* Jefferson, NC: McFarland & Company, Inc., Publishers, 2003.

Raines, Howell. *My Soul Is Rested: The Story of the Civil Rights Movement in the Deep South.* New York: Penguin, 1983.

Reporting Civil Rights. Vol.1, *American Journalism 1941–1963,* Library of America, 2003. Distributed by Penguin Putnam.

Roberts, Gene, and Hank Klibanoff. *Race Beat: The Press, the Civil Rights Struggle, and the Awakening of a Nation.* New York: Alfred A. Knopf, 2006.

Sitkoff, Harvard. *The Struggle for Black Equality, 1954–1992.* Revised ed. New York: Hill and Wang, 1993.

Weisbrot, Robert. *Freedom Bound: A History of America's Civil Rights Movement.* New York: W.W. Norton & Company, 1990.

Wexler, Sanford. *The Civil Rights Movement: An Eyewitness History.* New York: Facts On File, 1993.

Wolff, Miles. *Lunch at the Five and Ten: The Greensboro Sit-Ins, A Contemporary History.* New York: Stein and Day, 1970.

Zinn, Howard. *SNCC: The New Abolitionists.* Boston: Beacon Press, 1965.

Books

Bausum, Ann. *Freedom Riders*. Washington, D.C.: National Geographic, 2005.

Finlayson, Reggie. *We Shall Overcome: The History of the American Civil Rights Movement*. Minneapolis: Twenty-First Century Books, 2003.

Goldstein, Margaret. *America in the 1960s*. Minneapolis: Twenty-First Century Books, 2010.

Greene, Meg. *Into the Land of Freedom: African Americans in Reconstruction*. Minneapolis: Twenty-First Century Books, 2004.

Levine, Ellen S. *Freedom's Children*. New York: Putnam, 2000.

Manheimer, Ann S. *Martin Luther King Jr.: Dreaming of Equality*. Minneapolis: Twenty-First Century Books, 2005.

McWhorter, Diane. *A Dream of Freedom*. New York: Scholastic, 2004.

Morrison, Toni. *Remember: The Journey to School Integration*. Boston: Houghton Mifflin, 2004.

Partridge, Elizabeth. *Marching Toward Freedom*. New York: Viking Press, 2009.

Rochelle, Belinda. *Witnesses to Freedom*. New York: Puffin, 1997.

Time Inc. Home Entertainment Library. *LIFE: Remembering Martin Luther King, Jr.: His Life and Crusade in Pictures*. Minneapolis: Twenty-First Century Books, 2009.

Websites

The American Presidency Project
http://www.presidency.ucsb.edu
This is an archive of more than 80,000 documents about the American presidency, including speeches, policy statements, and presidential papers.

Civil Rights Movement Veterans
http://www.crmvet.org
A history of the civil rights movement in the United States is presented here, as well as photos from the period.

"Eyes on the Prize: America's Civil Rights Movement, 1954-1985" (PBS)
http://www.pbs.org/wgbh/amex/eyesontheprize/resources/index.html
This is a website connected to the PBS series *American Experience*, and this particular site presents material used in the program "Eyes on the Prize," about the American civil rights movement.

Greensboro VOICES: Voicing Observations in Civil Rights and Equality Struggles
http://library.uncg.edu/depts/archives/civrights/
This site contains oral histories from the people involved in the Greensboro sit-in of 1960, and other civil rights activities in Greensboro, North Carolina.

John F. Kennedy Link
http://www.jfklink.com
This is an archive of documents relating to the life, administration, death, and legacy of John F. Kennedy.

John F. Kennedy Presidential Library & Museum
http://www.jfklibrary.org
This is the site for the JFK archives and the JFK Library and Museum.

Martin Luther King, Jr. Research and Education Institute
http://mlk-kpp01.stanford.edu/
This site contains a collection of Martin Luther King Jr.'s papers and information about other civil rights figures.

National Civil Rights Museum
http://www.civilrightsmuseum.org
This museum is located at the Lorraine Motel in Nashville, Tennessee, where Martin Luther King Jr. was assassinated. The site contains links to other websites concerning the civil rights movement.

Separate Is Not Equal: *Brown v. Board of Education*
http://americanhistory.si.edu/brown/history
This is a Smithsonian Institution site that presents the story of *Brown vs. Board of Education* (1954).

We Shall Overcome: Historic Places of the Civil Rights Movement
http://www.cr.nps.gov/nr/travel/civilrights
A brief history of the civil rights movement, with descriptions of historic places, can be found on this site.

PHOTO ACKNOWLEDGMENTS

The images in this book are used with the permission of: © Jack Moebes/CORBIS, pp. 4, 37, 43, 46, 64, 67, 68, 84, 113; © Gabriel Benzur/Time & Life Pictures/Getty Images, p. 7; Independence National Historical Park, p. 8; © Bettmann/CORBIS, pp. 12, 58, 69, 73, 90–91, 106, 110 (both); AP Photo, pp. 14, 15, 76, 88, 94, 111, 117, 119, 122, 123, 129, 133, 134; Library of Congress, pp. 21 (LC-DIG-cwpb-02891), 32 (LC-USZ62-33783), 38 (LC-USZ62-41653), 51 (LC-USZ62-119154), 124 (LC-DIG-ppmsca-04295); © SuperStock/SuperStock, p. 22; © Lightfoot/Hulton Archive/Getty Images, p. 23; The Granger Collection, New York, pp. 24, 98; AP Photo/USAAF, p. 27; © Buyenlarge/Hulton Archive/Getty Images, p. 28; © Hank Walker/Time & Life Pictures/Getty Images, p. 34; © Paul Schutzer/Time & Life Pictures/Getty Images, p. 39; © Francis Miller/Time & Life Pictures/Getty Images, p. 48; © Carol W. Martin/Greensboro Historical Museum Collection, p. 52; © Mansell/Time & Life Pictures/Getty Images, p. 55; AP Photo/Gene Herrick, p. 56; © Don Cravens/Time & Life Pictures/Getty Images, p. 57; © News & Record by Staff Photographer, All Rights Reserved, pp. 60, 78, 85; Greensboro Historical Museum Archives, p. 62; © News & Record by Roy Matherly, Staff Photographer, All Rights Reserved, p. 83; © Laura Westlund/Independent Picture Service, p. 89; © Donald Uhrbrock/Time & Life Pictures/Getty Images, pp. 93, 126–127; AP Photo/Rudolph Faircloth, p. 95; © Cecil J. Williams, pp. 96, 97; AP Photo/Jack Harris, p. 102; © Walter Bennett/Time & Life Pictures/Getty Images, p. 104; © George Ballis/Take Stock/The Image Works, p. 109; © A.Y. Owen/Time & Life Pictures/Getty Images, p. 114; AP Photo/Byron Rollins, p. 125; AP Photo/Bill Hudson, p. 130; © AFP/AFP/Getty Images, p. 132; AP Photo/Chuck Burton, pp. 137, 139.

Front cover: © Jack Moebes/CORBIS.

ABOUT THE AUTHOR

Melody Herr, Ph.D., is a historian and a writer. In addition to several books on African American history, she has published both nonfiction and fiction about exploration and archaeology.